When you find you are drowning in your own life—working harder, sleeping less, putting out fires, filling your hours with to-dos, and enjoying very little of it—I pray that Erin Loechner's gentle, wise book will find its way into your hands. *Chasing Slow* guides us to a simpler life worth living. Prepare to feel your heart rate drop as you read these soothing, smart words.

> —**Gabrielle Blair,** mother of six; blogger; author,
> *New York Times* bestselling *Design Mom*

Erin's writing is beautiful, and this book is soulful and practical, honest and inspiring. For all of us who are tempted to perform and filter and prove—which is, I think, all of us—this is a necessary conversation about a deeper, better way of living.

> —**Shauna Niequist,** author, *Bread and Wine* and *Savor*

In the fast lane of life, this book is a much needed rest stop for th

> —**Bethany Joy Clark,** global brand ambassador, TOMS

Beautifully written. Beautifully lived. *Chasing Slow* will capture your attention, shift your perspective on life, and mark your journey as you move toward what matters.

> —**Ellie Holcomb,** singer/songwriter; Dove Award–winning artist

When the world yells, "Be more, run faster, try harder," I'll pick up this book again to remind me that true joy lies in the beauty of slow and present. With grace and humor, Erin tells the stories I need to hear and brought my heart back home.

> —**Kelle Hampton,** author, *New York Times* bestselling memoir *Bloom*

Erin Loechner has a calming presence, a reassuring voice, and a life-giving soul. You'll walk away from these pages shifted and feeling whole instead of hurried. Her words are a brave call to a fast-paced generation, and I cannot suggest reading them enough.

> —**Jess Connolly,** speaker; coauthor, *Wild and Free*

Reading *Chasing Slow* is like eating a really scrumptious meal that also happens to be good for you. Erin's voice is honest even when it hurts, inviting even when we don't deserve the invitation. I consumed this delicious, compelling book in a weekend and bled my highlighter dry along the way.

> —**Raechel Myers,** cofounder and CEO, She Reads Truth

Erin has always stood out as someone who knows how to get beyond the pretty picture and all the comments and likes of social media. In her eloquent, smart, and real story about the evolution of her online and offline journey, she reminds us how to accept ourselves, feel more with less, and soak up life as it come to us.

—**Joy Cho,** founder, Oh Joy!

Chasing Slow is equal parts memoir, meditation, and map to a more peaceful life. Erin Loechner has an artist's eye for beauty, a poet's ear for metaphor, and a scientist's mind for investigation and clarity. Her wise voice stayed with me long after I finished the book.

—**Asha Dornfest,** author, *Parent Hacks* and *Minimalist Parenting*

Erin takes us on a charming, meandering dance of stories, witticisms, and wisdoms. This book is for dreamers, adventurers, creatives, students, mamas, and professionals, but more than that, it's for those of us feeling flawed and desperately craving connection. I'm adding it to a very short stack of inspiring favorites, and cannot wait to read it again.

—**Whitney English,** founder and CEO, Day Designer

With four daughters and a job that I love, it is a great challenge for me to keep prioritized those things that give me true joy. As more activity comes into my life, Erin's story has given me not only inspiration but a practical framework to make healthy and easily implemented choices.

—**Barrett Ward,** CEO, FASHIONABLE

Erin's way of thinking shows the fruit of living slowly. She pulls at every string, peeks beneath every layer. She connects the dots of how so many of us are feeling, putting words to questions we're only just beginning to ask. This book is beautifully written, and you'll want to savor it.

—**Hayley Morgan,** coauthor, *Wild and Free*

CHASING SLOW

CHASING SLOW

CHASING SLOW

COURAGE TO JOURNEY OFF

THE BEATEN PATH

ERIN LOECHNER

ZONDERVAN
BOOKS

ZONDERVAN BOOKS

Chasing Slow
Copyright © 2016 by Erin Loechner

Published in Grand Rapids, Michigan, by Zondervan. Zondervan is a registered trademark of HarperCollins Christian Publishing, Inc.

Requests for information should be addressed to customercare@harpercollins.com.

Zondervan titles may be purchased in bulk for educational, business, fundraising, or sales promotional use. For information, please email SpecialMarkets@Zondervan.com.

ISBN 978-0-310-36876-2 (softcover)
ISBN 978-0-310-35016-3 (audio)
ISBN 978-0-310-34568-8 (ebook)

Library of Congress Cataloging-in-Publication Data

Names: Loechner, Erin, author.
Title: Chasing slow : courage to journey off the beaten path / Erin Loechner.
Description: Grand Rapids : Zondervan, 2017. | Includes bibliographical references.
Identifiers: LCCN 2016018055 | ISBN 9780310345671 (hardcover)
Subjects: LCSH: Simplicity--Religious aspects--Christianity. | Christian biography.
Classification: LCC BV4647.S48 L64 2017 | DDC 248.4--dc23 LC record available at https://lccn.loc.gov
   /2016018055

Scripture quotations are taken from The Holy Bible, New International Version®, NIV®. Copyright © 1973, 1978, 1984, 2011 by Biblica, Inc.® Used by permission of Zondervan. All rights reserved worldwide. www.Zondervan .com. The "NIV" and "New International Version" are trademarks registered in the United States Patent and Trademark Office by Biblica, Inc.®

Any internet addresses (websites, blogs, etc.) and telephone numbers in this book are offered as a resource. They are not intended in any way to be or imply an endorsement by Zondervan, nor does Zondervan vouch for the content of these sites and numbers for the life of this book.

All rights reserved. No part of this publication may be reproduced, stored in a retrieval system, or transmitted in any form or by any means—electronic, mechanical, photocopy, recording, or any other—except for brief quotations in printed reviews, without the prior permission of the publisher.

Art direction: Erin Loechner
Interior typesetting: Kait Lamphere
Cover and interior photos: Ken Loechner

Printed in the United States of America

HB 04.30.2024

This book is a work of creative nonfiction. This means I can write a true story about my life but still throw a dinner party and invite those whose names might have been changed.

So here it is. The truth as I've seen it.

FOR KEN

CONTENTS

PART THREE // SURRENDER

INTRO
DUCTION

WELCOME TO THE JUNGLE

Listen, are you breathing just a little, and calling it a life?
—Mary Oliver, "West Wind"

Sugar, let me give you some advice here."

I am nearly eighteen, at the DMV, posing for my first driver's license photo. It's back-to-school season, and Shelley, my appointed clerk, is wearing miniature pencil earrings and a school-bus-yellow sweater. As she speaks, I fixate on the tiny pencils, plus a Bic pen she has tucked behind her ear.

"You don't wanna smile too cute, 'kay?" she says. "Pity over pretty. Think about it, Sugar. You know who's gonna see this card? The cops, right before they bust you. You want 'em to feel a little bit sorry for you is all

I'm sayin'. Chin down, eyes up, no teeth—pitiful, you know?"

She pronounces it *pity-full*, and in my head I've pronounced it this way ever since. It seems right.

"You ready? One, two . . ."

On three, she and her pencil earrings snap the photo. As I gather my receipts, as I sign with her Bic pen, she says, "You did good on the photo, Sugar. Real good. Parallel parking needs some work, though."

I thank her, and I smile as I leave. For a moment, I wonder if Shelley is wrong about the photo. Shouldn't I have smiled wide with confidence? Eyes open, ready for the world? A happy, well-adjusted girl with a bright future?

That's who I am, right? Confident? Happy? Bright future?

Right?

Years later, my bright future takes me to Los Angeles.

Every Monday morning, when the early sun is a clementine, commuters line up bumper-to-bumper on the 405, all of us traveling through clogged arteries to the pulsating, thumping heart of it all: Hollywood.

L.A. – 2005

You have to call it that, *the* 405. It needs something to signify its importance to the inner workings of LA. *The* sun. *The* moon. *The* pope.

The first day I experience the 405, I still have cardboard boxes in my back seat. I am a college grad from Indiana, accustomed to little more than a four-lane highway. Traffic moves swiftly and I keep one eye fixed on my

directions, one eye fixed on the road ahead. I am driving to my new apartment, the one my filmmaker fiance, Ken, has found for me, the one I will be living in for the next few months until we marry.

To a small-town girl, the traffic is arduous, new. In my rusting Toyota Echo, I play Tom Petty and the Shins with the windows up, my eyes focused on the brake lights ahead. I wait. I watch. I pick at my cuticles. Mostly, I think about lunch.

We—the great commuters of LA—creep along, moving in patterns not unlike members of a band marching in step. We've never practiced together before, but somehow we know the routine: change lanes to the right, to the left, to the right with a jolt. There is a steady beat. Music. A mutually agreed-upon rhythm of slightly suppressed rage.

And then one artery opens, then another, and soon another, and the lanes branch, the 405 becoming a beast. Cars whoosh. Road signs zoom. Landmarks blur. Horns honk.

The beat becomes louder, faster, stronger. *Keep up*, it pounds.

My exit comes faster than I am prepared for, and as I flip on my turn signal and cross lanes, I see them in my rearview mirror: the flashing lights, the motorcycle, the officer.

With the siren blaring behind me, I exit slowly and veer into a gas station. I put the car in park and all is silent until I hear the officer's heavy steps approaching my car. He lowers his aviators and I can see that his face looks vaguely like my uncle Steve's, premustache.

"Ma'am," he starts, and this is when I burst into tears, movie-cliche style.

I cannot find my license, and I'm thinking of Shelley's advice, wondering what good the photo could possibly do me now. Surely I'm headed to the LA sheriff's department for an overnight stay until one of the three people I know in LA (and two of the three I met only yesterday) can bail me out. Isn't this what happens to disorganized drivers without documentation? Do Shelley's rules apply to a mug shot, I wonder? Do they serve coffee in jail? Can I call my mother to tell her, "Yes, yes, I am safe and sound but momentarily detained, and hey, while I've got you, is Aunt Beth's birthday today or Wednesday?"

I begin my explanation in tears, gulping of air. "I've just moved here from the Midwest," I say, pointing toward the boxes, and the officer stops me midsentence, midbreath, midtears, and smiles. "I can tell."

As Officer Not-Uncle-Steve explains my traffic violation, he tells me I haven't done anything wrong, technically. I have just been pulled over for driving too slowly, for exiting too leisurely.

"Honey, you're gonna need to pick up the pace if you're gonna make it out here. Just speed it up a bit. You'll be fine."

I blink back a few more tears and wipe my eyelids with a crinkled Starbucks napkin I'd found earlier (in my glove compartment, next to the mace). I am still overwhelmed, but I no longer feel like crying. I feel like understanding. Sometimes a simple change of the story, a quick line with a confusing twist, is just enough to surprise away the tears.

Driving too slowly? Exiting too leisurely? I didn't know this was possible.

This is not the last time I will realize that in LA, anything is possible.

He hands me a written warning and gives my car a few taps, the same kind my tuxedo-clad father-in-law, months later, will offer our getaway car on the night of my wedding. As the officer slides on his shades and walks back to his motorcycle, he shouts, "Welcome to the jungle!"

It has been said that the lion is king of the jungle. And while I no longer live there, in the jungle of LA, the lion has followed me ever since. I spent many years climbing trees, chasing tigers, conquering mountains. I worked and amassed, clawing at the dirt beneath me until it became a treacherous pit to contain all the more, more, more.

I grew faster, stronger, better. I learned that a few swipes of Essie Wrapped in Rubies nail polish can hide the dirt under my nails.

And the pit simply grew deeper, a bottomless hole.

When I left LA, when I escaped by the skin of my teeth, I assumed I left the lion behind. I had turned my back on the gnashing, the prowling, the hunger.

But lions are hunters. They will lurk, seeking to devour, and the words of poet and philosopher Friedrich Schiller can be caught on the tamest of winds:

"Did you think the lion was sleeping because he did not roar?"

There is a lion inside us all. It reigns over pace and time and intention, and it lingers in the rooms of our hearts daily. It roams, searching for the reasons we were placed on this planet—our passions, dreams, abilities—and it scoffs at the demands of our daily lives—our schedules, responsibilities.

Do you hear it? The silence?

Do you feel it? The roaming?

But a lion is unruly. It cannot be trusted, can it? Just look at that mane, those teeth, that jaw.

So we attempt to tame it.

We fill our lion's den with productivity apps that offer us more time, which we use to find more time-saving productivity apps. We fill it with geometric vases to match Pantone's It Color of the Year, with a new pair of boyfriend jeans, with a first-class upgrade on a snowy flight to Salt Lake City. We fill it with another kale recipe that uses six ingredients to make kale taste not so much like kale. And have you tried eyelash extensions? You'll look like you've slept seven and a half hours. At least!

We fluff this great pit with our ego boosts, our need for control, our unrealistic expectations, and soon our days are dictated by its excess. The lion sulks around our soul, pacing for his next meal, hungry for more than we are throwing his way.

Perhaps we are feeding him the wrong thing.

What would our lion, once his den emptied, hunt down within us? What would he discover hidden in the twisted jungles of our minds? What might he whisper?

Could he roar again?

I have been filling my den, for many years, with more—more stuff, more scheduling, more speed, more status.

And I believe it is time to offer less.

A lion is a hunter, after all, and a hunter cannot be tamed. It's probably best to clear the path of distractions.

This book is an ongoing chase with my own lion. I'm writing it from my jungle, fingers to the keyboard, a hunter at my heels.

Quiet now; he is stirring.

Come.

This way.

I know a shortcut.

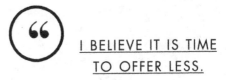

I BELIEVE IT IS TIME
TO OFFER LESS.

When you find you are drowning in your own life—working harder, sleeping less, putting out fires, filling your hours with to-dos, and enjoying very little of it—I pray that Erin Loechner's gentle, wise book will find its way into your hands. *Chasing Slow* guides us to a simpler life worth living. Prepare to feel your heart rate drop as you read these soothing, smart words.

> —**Gabrielle Blair,** mother of six; blogger; author,
> *New York Times* bestselling *Design Mom*

Erin's writing is beautiful, and this book is soulful and practical, honest and inspiring. For all of us who are tempted to perform and filter and prove—which is, I think, all of us—this is a necessary conversation about a deeper, better way of living.

> —**Shauna Niequist,** author, *Bread and Wine* and *Savor*

In the fast lane of life, this book is a much needed rest stop for the soul.

> —**Bethany Joy Clark,** global brand ambassador, TOMS

Beautifully written. Beautifully lived. *Chasing Slow* will capture your attention, shift your perspective on life, and mark your journey as you move toward what matters.

> —**Ellie Holcomb,** singer/songwriter; Dove Award–winning artist

When the world yells, "Be more, run faster, try harder," I'll pick up this book again to remind me that true joy lies in the beauty of slow and present. With grace and humor, Erin tells the stories I need to hear and brought my heart back home.

> —**Kelle Hampton,** author, *New York Times* bestselling memoir *Bloom*

Erin Loechner has a calming presence, a reassuring voice, and a life-giving soul. You'll walk away from these pages shifted and feeling whole instead of hurried. Her words are a brave call to a fast-paced generation, and I cannot suggest reading them enough.

> —**Jess Connolly,** speaker; coauthor, *Wild and Free*

Reading *Chasing Slow* is like eating a really scrumptious meal that also happens to be good for you. Erin's voice is honest even when it hurts, inviting even when we don't deserve the invitation. I consumed this delicious, compelling book in a weekend and bled my highlighter dry along the way.

> —**Raechel Myers,** cofounder and CEO, She Reads Truth

Erin has always stood out as someone who knows how to get beyond the pretty picture and all the comments and likes of social media. In her eloquent, smart, and real story about the evolution of her online and offline journey, she reminds us how to accept ourselves, feel more with less, and soak up life as it come to us.

—**Joy Cho,** founder, Oh Joy!

Chasing Slow is equal parts memoir, meditation, and map to a more peaceful life. Erin Loechner has an artist's eye for beauty, a poet's ear for metaphor, and a scientist's mind for investigation and clarity. Her wise voice stayed with me long after I finished the book.

—**Asha Dornfest,** author, *Parent Hacks* and *Minimalist Parenting*

Erin takes us on a charming, meandering dance of stories, witticisms, and wisdoms. This book is for dreamers, adventurers, creatives, students, mamas, and professionals, but more than that, it's for those of us feeling flawed and desperately craving connection. I'm adding it to a very short stack of inspiring favorites, and cannot wait to read it again.

—**Whitney English,** founder and CEO, Day Designer

With four daughters and a job that I love, it is a great challenge for me to keep prioritized those things that give me true joy. As more activity comes into my life, Erin's story has given me not only inspiration but a practical framework to make healthy and easily implemented choices.

—**Barrett Ward,** CEO, FASHION**ABLE**

Erin's way of thinking shows the fruit of living slowly. She pulls at every string, peeks beneath every layer. She connects the dots of how so many of us are feeling, putting words to questions we're only just beginning to ask. This book is beautifully written, and you'll want to savor it.

—**Hayley Morgan,** coauthor, *Wild and Free*

CHASING SLOW

CHASING SLOW

COURAGE TO JOURNEY OFF

THE BEATEN PATH

ERIN LOECHNER

ZONDERVAN BOOKS

ZONDERVAN BOOKS

Chasing Slow
Copyright © 2016 by Erin Loechner

Published in Grand Rapids, Michigan, by Zondervan. Zondervan is a registered trademark of HarperCollins Christian Publishing, Inc.

Requests for information should be addressed to customercare@harpercollins.com.

Zondervan titles may be purchased in bulk for educational, business, fundraising, or sales promotional use. For information, please email SpecialMarkets@Zondervan.com.

ISBN 978-0-310-36876-2 (softcover)
ISBN 978-0-310-35016-3 (audio)
ISBN 978-0-310-34568-8 (ebook)

Library of Congress Cataloging-in-Publication Data

Names: Loechner, Erin, author.
Title: Chasing slow : courage to journey off the beaten path / Erin Loechner.
Description: Grand Rapids : Zondervan, 2017. | Includes bibliographical references.
Identifiers: LCCN 2016018055 | ISBN 9780310345671 (hardcover)
Subjects: LCSH: Simplicity--Religious aspects--Christianity. | Christian biography.
Classification: LCC BV4647.S48 L64 2017 | DDC 248.4--dc23 LC record available at https://lccn.loc.gov
    /2016018055

Scripture quotations are taken from The Holy Bible, New International Version®, NIV®. Copyright © 1973, 1978, 1984, 2011 by Biblica, Inc.® Used by permission of Zondervan. All rights reserved worldwide. www.Zondervan .com. The "NIV" and "New International Version" are trademarks registered in the United States Patent and Trademark Office by Biblica, Inc.®

Any internet addresses (websites, blogs, etc.) and telephone numbers in this book are offered as a resource. They are not intended in any way to be or imply an endorsement by Zondervan, nor does Zondervan vouch for the content of these sites and numbers for the life of this book.

All rights reserved. No part of this publication may be reproduced, stored in a retrieval system, or transmitted in any form or by any means—electronic, mechanical, photocopy, recording, or any other—except for brief quotations in printed reviews, without the prior permission of the publisher.

Art direction: Erin Loechner
Interior typesetting: Kait Lamphere
Cover and interior photos: Ken Loechner

Printed in the United States of America

HB 04.30.2024

This book is a work of creative nonfiction. This means I can write a true story about my life but still throw a dinner party and invite those whose names might have been changed.

So here it is. The truth as I've seen it.

FOR KEN

CONTENTS

PART THREE // SURRENDER

INTRO
DUCTION

WELCOME TO THE JUNGLE

Listen, are you breathing just a little, and calling it a life?
—*Mary Oliver, "West Wind"*

Sugar, let me give you some advice here."

I am nearly eighteen, at the DMV, posing for my first driver's license photo. It's back-to-school season, and Shelley, my appointed clerk, is wearing miniature pencil earrings and a school-bus-yellow sweater. As she speaks, I fixate on the tiny pencils, plus a Bic pen she has tucked behind her ear.

"You don't wanna smile too cute, 'kay?" she says. "Pity over pretty. Think about it, Sugar. You know who's gonna see this card? The cops, right before they bust you. You want 'em to feel a little bit sorry for you is all

I'm sayin'. Chin down, eyes up, no teeth—pitiful, you know?"

She pronounces it *pity-full*, and in my head I've pronounced it this way ever since. It seems right.

"You ready? One, two . . ."

On three, she and her pencil earrings snap the photo. As I gather my receipts, as I sign with her Bic pen, she says, "You did good on the photo, Sugar. Real good. Parallel parking needs some work, though."

I thank her, and I smile as I leave. For a moment, I wonder if Shelley is wrong about the photo. Shouldn't I have smiled wide with confidence? Eyes open, ready for the world? A happy, well-adjusted girl with a bright future?

That's who I am, right? Confident? Happy? Bright future?

Right?

Years later, my bright future takes me to Los Angeles.

−A. − 2005

Every Monday morning, when the early sun is a clementine, commuters line up bumper-to-bumper on the 405, all of us traveling through clogged arteries to the pulsating, thumping heart of it all: Hollywood.

You have to call it that, *the* 405. It needs something to signify its importance to the inner workings of LA. *The* sun. *The* moon. *The* pope.

The first day I experience the 405, I still have cardboard boxes in my back seat. I am a college grad from Indiana, accustomed to little more than a four-lane highway. Traffic moves swiftly and I keep one eye fixed on my directions, one eye fixed on the road ahead. I am driving to my new apartment, the one my filmmaker fiance, Ken, has found for me, the one I will be living in for the next few months until we marry.

To a small-town girl, the traffic is arduous, new. In my rusting Toyota Echo, I play Tom Petty and the Shins with the windows up, my eyes focused on the brake lights ahead. I wait. I watch. I pick at my cuticles. Mostly, I think about lunch.

We—the great commuters of LA—creep along, moving in patterns not unlike members of a band marching in step. We've never practiced together before, but somehow we know the routine: change lanes to the right, to the left, to the right with a jolt. There is a steady beat. Music. A mutually agreed-upon rhythm of slightly suppressed rage.

And then one artery opens, then another, and soon another, and the lanes branch, the 405 becoming a beast. Cars whoosh. Road signs zoom. Landmarks blur. Horns honk.

The beat becomes louder, faster, stronger. *Keep up,* it pounds.

My exit comes faster than I am prepared for, and as I flip on my turn signal and cross lanes, I see them in my rearview mirror: the flashing lights, the motorcycle, the officer.

With the siren blaring behind me, I exit slowly and veer into a gas station. I put the car in park and all is silent until I hear the officer's heavy steps approaching my car. He lowers his aviators and I can see that his face looks vaguely like my uncle Steve's, premustache.

"Ma'am," he starts, and this is when I burst into tears, movie-cliché style.

I cannot find my license, and I'm thinking of Shelley's advice, wondering what good the photo could possibly do me now. Surely I'm headed to the LA sheriff's department for an overnight stay until one of the three people I know in LA (and two of the three I met only yesterday) can bail me out. Isn't this what happens to disorganized drivers without documentation? Do Shelley's rules apply to a mug shot, I wonder? Do they serve coffee in jail? Can I call my mother to tell her, "Yes, yes, I am safe and sound but momentarily detained, and hey, while I've got you, is Aunt Beth's birthday today or Wednesday?"

I begin my explanation in tears, gulping of air. "I've just moved here from the Midwest," I say, pointing toward the boxes, and the officer stops me midsentence, midbreath, midtears, and smiles. "I can tell."

As Officer Not-Uncle-Steve explains my traffic violation, he tells me I haven't done anything wrong, technically. I have just been pulled over for driving too slowly, for exiting too leisurely.

"Honey, you're gonna need to pick up the pace if you're gonna make it out here. Just speed it up a bit. You'll be fine."

I blink back a few more tears and wipe my eyelids with a crinkled Starbucks napkin I'd found earlier (in my glove compartment, next to the mace). I am still overwhelmed, but I no longer feel like crying. I feel like understanding. Sometimes a simple change of the story, a quick line with a confusing twist, is just enough to surprise away the tears.

Driving too slowly? Exiting too leisurely? I didn't know this was possible.

This is not the last time I will realize that in LA, anything is possible.

He hands me a written warning and gives my car a few taps, the same kind my tuxedo-clad father-in-law, months later, will offer our getaway car on the night of my wedding. As the officer slides on his shades and walks back to his motorcycle, he shouts, "Welcome to the jungle!"

It has been said that the lion is king of the jungle. And while I no longer live there, in the jungle of LA, the lion has followed me ever since. I spent many years climbing trees, chasing tigers, conquering mountains. I worked and amassed, clawing at the dirt beneath me until it became a treacherous pit to contain all the more, more, more.

I grew faster, stronger, better. I learned that a few swipes of Essie Wrapped in Rubies nail polish can hide the dirt under my nails.

And the pit simply grew deeper, a bottomless hole.

When I left LA, when I escaped by the skin of my teeth, I assumed I left the lion behind. I had turned my back on the gnashing, the prowling, the hunger.

But lions are hunters. They will lurk, seeking to devour, and the words of poet and philosopher Friedrich Schiller can be caught on the tamest of winds:

"Did you think the lion was sleeping because he did not roar?"

There is a lion inside us all. It reigns over pace and time and intention, and it lingers in the rooms of our hearts daily. It roams, searching for the reasons we were placed on this planet—our passions, dreams, abilities—and it scoffs at the demands of our daily lives—our schedules, responsibilities.

Do you hear it? The silence?

Do you feel it? The roaming?

But a lion is unruly. It cannot be trusted, can it? Just look at that mane, those teeth, that jaw.

So we attempt to tame it.

We fill our lion's den with productivity apps that offer us more time, which we use to find more time-saving productivity apps. We fill it with geometric vases to match Pantone's It Color of the Year, with a new pair of boyfriend jeans, with a first-class upgrade on a snowy flight to Salt Lake City. We fill it with another kale recipe that uses six ingredients to make kale taste not so much like kale. And have you tried eyelash extensions? You'll look like you've slept seven and a half hours. At least!

We fluff this great pit with our ego boosts, our need for control, our unrealistic expectations, and soon our days are dictated by its excess. The lion sulks around our soul, pacing for his next meal, hungry for more than we are throwing his way.

Perhaps we are feeding him the wrong thing.

What would our lion, once his den emptied, hunt down within us? What would he discover hidden in the twisted jungles of our minds? What might he whisper?

Could he roar again?

I have been filling my den, for many years, with more—more stuff, more scheduling, more speed, more status.

And I believe it is time to offer less.

A lion is a hunter, after all, and a hunter cannot be tamed. It's probably best to clear the path of distractions.

This book is an ongoing chase with my own lion. I'm writing it from my jungle, fingers to the keyboard, a hunter at my heels.

Quiet now; he is stirring.

Come.

This way.

I know a shortcut.

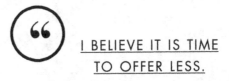

I BELIEVE IT IS TIME
TO OFFER LESS.

CHASING MORE

1

100

1.

A LIFE OF QUESTION MARKS

They say a person needs just three things to be truly happy in this world:
someone to love, something to do, and something to hope for.
—*Tom Bodett*

I married a man with an expiration date. "Thirty," the doctor had said. "He might live to be thirty."

His name is Ken. We had not intended to marry, or even to stick around for dinner, as all great love stories go. It was a surprise beginning more than a decade ago, both of us hopelessly preoccupied elsewhere until those elsewheres collided filming a documentary in an aged, towering mansion off-campus in middle America.

We had been handpicked with thirteen other college students to produce educational films for nonprofits. For five months we were part of an immersion course—we ate, slept, and edited footage in a large manor donated to the university. Leather sofas and marbled conservatories, chandeliers and velvet draperies—all were a far cry from our cinderblock dormrooms—and yet what I remember most is him.

Ken is older than me, with green eyes and a good voice. He wears a stocking cap when it is not cold, and at first glance, I am unimpressed. He is attractive, yes, but he is also intensely focused on his film career.

He has just won a regional Emmy. He is on the rise, skyrocketing on a trajectory that, in three short months, will drop him in the center of Hollywood. I am focused on growing out my bangs.

This is not to say that I don't take my studies seriously. I do, very much so. But I find myself continually searching, exploring, grasping for some level of understanding, for a hint of purpose beyond my 11:00 a.m. geography course. I join countless Bible studies. I fill my calendar with social activities, with late-night pizzas, with weekend frisbee in the quad. I find happiness, momentary fulfillment.

And then I find myself in the drugstore aisle choosing an improved skincare system—less acne, guaranteed, for $34.99! (My income from waitressing on the weekends isn't enough to justify the splurge, regardless of the value of improved skincare and the promise of a life transformed by a spotless T-zone.)

I find myself hanging twinkle lights over my loft instead of studying for my Spanish final.

I find myself peering at Greek-lettered students or blazer-clad professors, thinking, Does everyone else know what they're sup-posed to be doing? Is this making sense? Am I on the right page?

What am I looking for?

It is a cold February night, and tonight I have found myself in the mansion's living room logging footage and transcribing interviews for the documentaries of two local nonprofit organizations. It is late, and we're the last students to finish for the night, and so Ken asks what we both want to ask:

"Dinner?"

Soon we are in the tiled kitchen chopping mushrooms for a recipe only he knows by heart. He rinses parsley as he speaks of his sister; I mince garlic as I talk of mine. I ask about his favorite music as the water boils, and by the time the steam rises and the ziti has softened, we are on to religion, political views—chatting and learning, spanning decades in one night. As I drain the pasta, as he layers the ingredients into a baking dish, as I spread a final row of mozzarella on top and place the dish into the oven, I am no longer thinking of dinner.

Truly, the pasta turns out to be terrible. It burned as we lost ourselves in each other's words—distracted, engrossed, afraid, exhilarated. And somewhere between preheating

A FAR BETTER PASTA RECIPE
GARLIC ALFREDO ZUCCHINI PASTA

Alfredo Sauce Ingredients

1/2 cup raw cashews

1 medium white onion, chopped

4 garlic cloves, minced

1/2 cup olive oil

1/4 cup nutritional yeast

1 Tbsp lemon juice

1 cup vegetable broth

"Noodle" Ingredients

1 zucchini

001. Soak the raw cashews in 1/2 cup of water for 3 to 4 hours, then drain.

002. "Spiralize" the zucchini to create long, thin "pasta" pieces, then boil for 8 minutes over medium–high heat. If you don't have a spiralizer (Mom, just get one already), try a black bean spaghetti, or whatever, really. This part isn't important; the sauce is the main squeeze. Put it on a spoon, I don't care.

003. Cook the onion and garlic in the olive oil for 6 to 8 minutes or until browned. Or until you get too hungry. Whichever comes first.

004. Add the browned onion and garlic to a high-power blender (Mom, just get this one already too), along with the nutritional yeast, lemon juice, drained cashews, and vegetable broth. Blend on high for 30 seconds or on a sauce/broth setting.

005. Serve over zucchini noodles with halved cherry tomatoes and a bit of basil.

006. Lick the leftover sauce from the pan. This part is mandatory.

the oven and scraping the pan, we fell in love.

I hesitate to call it love, because it sounds trite and dramatic, but life is both of these things, sometimes in equal parts, and so I'm calling it: it was love.

Here is what I remember. I am sitting in a kitchen on a butcher-block countertop next to the sink, and I am positioned as a kindergartner, crisscross-applesauce style. He is leaning effortlessly against a cast-iron oven that, when heated, smells of forgotten pizzas and rust. My legs begin to fall asleep, begin to numb, begin to get prickly, but he is still telling that story and his laugh is so beautiful and his eyes, they are fixed on me, and if I move, will his gaze follow? Will I break the spell? I dare not move.

I shared this recollection at a dinner party once, and Ken, surprised, having never heard this, remembered his discomfort that night. Sweat had been trickling down the backs of his thighs—the oven he was leaning on heated more than our dinner—but we were powerless, really.

Sometimes the most holy thing we can do is to be still. To sit down and twirl the fork and eat the pasta we're given.

"Could you ever live in Los Angeles?" he asks me two months later over hotdogs. We are back in the mansion's kitchen, having just wrapped final projects for the year. He and his Emmy will leave for Hollywood in a week; I will finish school and serve margaritas to gentlemen in cowboy hats.

I search for hot sauce as Ken chops the most miniscule onions only a perfectionist could muster the patience for, and when he slices whole dill pickles lengthwise to create the consummate topper, I think, Vertical pickles! How creative! How ingenious! How very like him, I learned later. I'd never thought of taking the time for vertical pickles. In hotdogs, they make all the difference.

I haven't yet answered his question, and

 SOMETIMES THE MOST HOLY THING WE CAN DO IS TO BE STILL. TO SIT DOWN AND TWIRL THE FORK AND EAT THE PASTA WE'RE GIVEN.

my mind skips to the path that lies before me. Does Los Angeles fit? Can it? College graduation is still a few years away for me, but then I'll apply to graduate school, a hopeful professor of English literature or communications or new media. I want an office on campus, a tiny brick house I can bike home to for a lunch of tuna on rye. I want to grade papers in the evenings as I sip chilled wine and listen to Dean Martin, a trusty dog at my feet. I want to hear the neighbor kids jumping in crisp orange leaves. I want Indiana. I want my own plans.

Does California even have crisp orange leaves?

I have been raised to be an independent thinker, to have plans that don't revolve around the necessity of a romantic partner. Once, when watching *Grease* as a child, my mother came into the living room with a laundry basket on her hip to find her three daughters gyrating in imaginary leather pants to the closing number, "You're the One That I Want." Sandra Dee was standing there on the antennaed TV, mindboggling in that killer black outfit, cigarette in mouth, and my mother slammed down the laundry basket at our feet and said, "Fold the whites. And don't you dare ever change for a man."

I won't change who I am for Ken, I think. But I might be willing to change my zip code for him. Sometimes it's hard to see the difference between change and compromise, between sacrificing something you want for something you want a little bit more.

"I could live in Los Angeles," I say, "with you."

"I have a brain tumor," he said. My memory places this conversation on the same night as the hotdogs—was it really?—and in truth, I'm fuzzy on the details. I simply know that loving Ken, from the very beginning, has meant loving Ken-with-a-Brain-Tumor, and so I chose it. I chose them both.

It was perhaps naivete. It was perhaps selfishness to think that a short life with him was enough for me, that I didn't need to grow old with the one I loved, that old was a matter of mechanics anyway.

But I think it was young love, that's all.

When news spread that I'd chosen to marry Ken, that I'd signed up for a life of question marks—how long? when will? what if?—I simply took the logical approach: Aren't we all marrying a dying spouse? Aren't we all en route to the same destination?

What's forever to a twenty-year-old?

THE REASONS I SAID YES

Here's what I have: the reasons that this marriage, our California, could work:

001. Because when I cried on your white T-shirt that morning, tiny black butterflies of mascara stayed on your shoulder, and they never came out in the wash. Because you wore it anyway, even though the smudges made your shirt look dirty. Because you laughed as you suggested I try waterproof.

002. Because you wrote my name on your grocery list.

003. Because of the night we shared fried rice in the park, when the fireflies had come out, and what was it you'd said about the trees? That they were older than us, older than life? Strong but breakable but standing here, nearly forever?

004. Because you never once rolled your eyes when a waitress mispronounced *espresso*.

005. Because you laughed without judgment when I confessed that, all along, I'd thought it was Oreo Speedwagon.

006. Because California has bikes and tuna and chilled wine and neighbor kids. Crisp orange leaves? California has clementines. And mostly it would have you.

007. Because of what happened next.

There were doubts, certainly.

Could I learn to fold his T-shirts the way his mother had, without the middle crease? Could he rap the words to Vanilla Ice when I needed a smile? Could I remember to wrap the leftover pizza in foil? Could he be bothered to take out the trash?

Could we make it not as dying man and living woman but as husband and wife?

In sickness and in health, the vows read.

I agreed to one, and I told myself the other didn't matter.

The brain tumor—a glioma—is inoperable, and we are meant to keep an eye on it. It occurs to me that this is the silliest medical advice I have yet heard: to keep an eye on it. As if the brain tumor were a boiling pot or a checking-account balance. As if we didn't already have both eyes on it, as if it weren't a song on repeat, as if it weren't a catch in our throats, as if it weren't raining in our hearts.

I was once told by a doctor to keep an eye on a mole. It sits there, Ohio shaped, just under my left toenail, unchanging. It has not yet grown or moved, and so I dutifully, diligently, earnestly keep an eye on it. When the seasons turn and it is summer and I grab my grandmother's huarache sandals, I place the shoe on my foot and spread the woven leather just so to make a measurable window over the mole. Has it had a growth spurt? Was it always there in the top third row, just above the buckle? Does it still fit in its little leather window? Mostly, I keep an eye on how it is not changing, not one bit, how it is still there, still menacing, still branded onto my skin.

And in turn, it keeps an eye on me. An Ohio-sized reminder impeding my desire for control.

I want an answer. I want a roadmap, an equation, a resource page at the back of a book. I want to flip to the end of the story and see my favorite characters still altogether lovely and complete.

Years later, I (unwisely) google the latest glioma statistics and find a less than optimistic prognosis.

Gliomas are rarely curable. Of ten thousand Americans diagnosed each year with malignant gliomas, about half are alive one year after diagnosis, and 25 percent after two years.

Ken is brushing his teeth in the bathroom, and I sneak in from our dimly lit office to interrupt his gargling with a question: "What kind is your glioma called? Low level?"

He spits. "Low grade. Why?"

"Just curious," I say, handing him a washcloth to dab the toothpaste off his chin. I dash back to the office, the desktop computer screen aglow, my typing fingers leading the search with newfound information.

For low-grade tumors, the prognosis is somewhat more optimistic. Patients diagnosed with a low-grade glioma are seventeen times as likely to die as matched patients in the general population. The age-standardized ten-year relative survival rate is 47 percent. One study reported that low-grade oligodendroglioma patients have a median survival of 11.6 years; another reported a median survival of 16.7 years.

A MEDIAN SURVIVAL RATE OF 11.6 YEARS. IN MATH, YOU'D ROUND UP TO TWELVE. IN LIFE, DO YOU GET TO DO THE SAME?

10/1

Outside, the moon is high. I wonder about the decimal points in statistics, about this meticulous system of measurement.

A median survival rate of 11.6 years. In math, you'd round up to twelve. In life, do you get to do the same?

Ken and I marry on a warm October night in a blue hour during a candlelit service.

I almost missed the ceremony. My nephew had a soccer game I wanted to watch, and we hit construction traffic on the forty-five-minute ride home, detouring past cornfields and red barns, silos and the occasional gas station. There was just enough time to position the veil.

In our vows, I speak of Ken as being the kind of man who unwraps a pack of Starbursts on an airplane and sets aside all of the pink ones for you. They are your favorite, after all.

(You'd have married him too.)

In a champagne dress in my childhood church, while hot wax dances down the ivory tapered candles and splashes onto the stone altar below, I promise to love him through the expiration date he has been given.

A day, a month, 11.6 years, or a thousand years beyond.

Another report places the median survival rate at 16.7 years.

The night prior, we'd spent an hour or two lining the top of the altar with aluminum foil to protect the stone—it had been in the church since my parents' wedding decades before—but the wax spilled over it shortly after the flower girl approached the aisle, and for the rest of the ceremony, tiny stalactites dripped down, down, down to the carpet.

My father and uncles leave the reception early to scrape it off with pocket knives and credit cards. "It's what we do," they say when we protest, Ken portioning slices of cake for them into styrofoam takeout containers.

We thank them, and then we dance.

The only song I can remember is the one our DJ chose for our first dance. We didn't have a song yet, not really, not unless you count the top-forty hit we often hummed while faux waltzing around the kitchen floor, but certainly that doesn't qualify as a wedding song? Certainly we couldn't call it ours?

And so it was decided: "What a Wonderful World" by Louis Armstrong.

"It's nice. And it's short," the DJ said. "You'll want it to be short."

We spend our honeymoon sick with colds in Indiana, passing the tissue box back and forth on my parents' foldout sofa. We find ourselves opening a gift and pausing to blow our noses or to nap, and a short week later, we pile the rest of the gifts into our suitcases and leave for Los Angeles—for a new city, for an adventure, for a lifetime of youth. He holds the boarding passes; I hold his hand.

On the descent to LAX, Ken gets a headache from the pressure. "Are you okay?" I ask. "Are you going to be okay?"

I am not asking Ken. I am asking God.

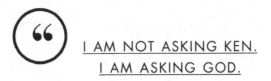

I AM NOT ASKING KEN.
I AM ASKING GOD.

00

2.

A SECRET PRAYER OF SORTS

God has given you one face, and you make yourself another.
—William Shakespeare

I have been asking God, keeping count, learning math all of my life.

I was raised in church, the one with the stone altar, seated in hard pews and singing from dusty red hymnals. If I squint, I can smell the wrinkled paper in the hymnals, infused with the sweat and faith of hundreds of hands. When the congregation turns to "Amazing Grace," I see a red line slashed down the middle of the page—a young tot's coloring gone awry, I imagine—and it makes verse 2 harder to read through the crayon wax.

T'was Grace that taught my heart to fear.
And Grace, my fears relieved.

My uncle and grandmother were the song leaders. I thought they were famous. I thought anyone with a microphone, anyone seated in the front of a church, anyone wearing a tie clip was famous.

I have always believed in God. There is something deep within me that seeks meaning, that rejects the idea we've been placed here to wander with no purpose, for no reason, for no significance.

But there is a moment in my childhood that derails me, a happening that now makes me laugh at dinner parties, but then did not make me laugh. It planted in me a

A SHORT LIST OF CHILDHOOD TRANSGRESSIONS

001. Punching my best friend in the stomach in kindergarten
002. Etching Wayne Lindford's initials into the bowling alley bathroom door
003. Tearing the heads off of my sister's J.C. Penney paper dolls
004. Putting gum in Keisha Falk's Barbie's hair
005. Putting gum in Keisha Falk's hair
006. Putting gum in my hair
007. Stealing gum
008. Stealing Jen Goshman's boyfriend

YOUR TURN?

garden of guilt I could not explain away, a row of unanswerable questions, a crop of unquestionable doubt.

It is summer camp, and I am a young preteen, and we've had what Christians like to call an "altar call" after outdoor worship, which is where the popular kids approach a tree-lined canopy in their neon windbreakers to confess underage drinking and premarital sex, and the others stay seated in the itchy grass, retying their boat shoes and adjusting their newly acquired friendship bracelets, trying to conjure up equally dramatic reasons to feel guilty and repent. My cousin Megan once told me that she confessed to the day we put sewing pins into our grandmother's seat cushion, and that she felt convicted and forgiven enough for the both of us. (I have not yet visited the altar for that infraction, so I'll say it now: sorry, Grandma.)

I am emotionally stirred and drained after a long week of marshmallows and Capture the Flag, and so I approach the altar trees for something else.

And it is here that a well-meaning, well-hairsprayed counselor asks why I am crying.

I am crying about something I can't put my finger on. I am crying because I don't understand what I am supposed to feel about this big, messy, ambiguous life. I am crying because I do not feel peaceful. I do not feel settled. I do not feel perfected. I do not feel transformed.

Am I not a Christian? What if I don't have Jesus in my heart? What if I am not truly saved? What if my baptism in fourth grade—I wore the striped dress from Osh-Kosh B'gosh to my banquet—what if it hadn't worked? Where is the joy we sing about in the hymnals? Where is the peace? Where is God?

You can see here how this story hinges on the counselor's reply, on her telling me the right thing at the right moment, movie-scene style.

But I am told the wrong thing, because there is always a wrong thing, and there is also an even more wrong thing. And sometimes finding the difference between the two is the only right thing there is.

I am told that there is a prayer, a secret prayer of sorts, and that if I don't recite it, I am not truly a Christian. It states that I am a sinner, separated from God, and I need forgiveness, and if I confess that Jesus is Lord and accept him into my heart, I will be saved—saved from myself, from my sins, from my humanness. If I accept him into my heart, he

will accept me into his. I will be transformed in the name of Jesus Christ, amen.

We are meant to keep an eye on it.

But the kicker is that this confessional, this sinner's prayer, is to be recited each and every time I sin.

T'was Grace that taught my heart to fear.

I don't know what to make of this deal-sealer now that I think of it years later—I am cringing at its mechanics—because at the time, it sounds so elementary. Easy enough, I think, until I realize how often I sin knowingly, and surely there are more times I have sinned unknowingly—I had, after all, coveted Casey's french braid multiple times that morning—and what will happen if I sin and promptly die before I finish reciting the prayer? Over a hairstyle, even. What if I don't get all the way to amen? What will I become? Where will I end up?

Hell, to be sure.

It is hell, to be sure.

I live the rest of my childhood looking over my shoulder, collecting sins from the day and tossing them into my bedtime prayers each night. While others count sheep, I count transgressions, and when I reach the hundreds, I roll over and turn off the bedside lamp, emptied.

These dark nights are the first memory I have of feeling unworthy, of feeling less than. Less than a good Christian girl. Less than a good Christian. Less than good.

And although I was never great at math—my dear, sweet principal Mr. Powell was enlisted to tutor me in subtraction while my second-grade classmates played Four Square at recess—I knew enough to assume a basic mathematical principle: if you feel less, add more.

Indian film producer Salman Khan perhaps said it best: "A lion runs the fastest when he is hungry."

So I ran.

With every accolade and accomplishment, with every trophy and ribbon, with every certificate and award, I was praised. Good became a noun. Good was a point of arrival. Being good was more important than becoming good, and when I fell short of the being, I bloodied my knuckles crawling back to the top.

When I was a freshman in high school, I tried out for the tennis team. For a week in spring, when the magnolias began to bloom, I lined up next to leggy blondes in Adidas track shorts as we practiced our swings on the olive-green courts.

Tennis was not a popular activity for my small-town peers, but I'd chosen it because I'd received a racket for Christmas—my mother had played and would I like her to teach me?—and the scent of new tennis balls was an aphrodisiac that seduced me into new territory. Perhaps this would be the newest court over which I'd reign. Perhaps this would be the addition to tip my scale from less to more.

There was another reason, of course. It was not a popular sport, which meant the stakes were low. I couldn't possibly fail, and if I did, there wouldn't be an audience to see it.

We spent the first week working on our backhands, our serves, our deep shots. After practice, a neighbor with her driver's license drove me home as she filled me in on months of tennis gossip. Just last year, a wrestler had

WHILE OTHERS COUNT SHEEP, I COUNT TRANSGRESSIONS, AND WHEN I REACH THE HUNDREDS, I ROLL OVER AND TURN OFF THE BEDSIDE LAMP, EMPTIED.

lost a bet and streaked on the court during cooldown.

"Coach ended practice fast, screaming at us to pick up the balls!" she told me, laughing. "Pick up the balls?! We just died."

I liked being part of the tennis team. I liked being the new girl, the one who didn't get the inside jokes, the special one who needed extra attention, additional explanations.

Friday afternoon, after a grueling set of agility drills, the coach pulled me aside with a whisper and a tap. We both were aware of the dozens of eyes upon us, my fellow pony-tailed classmates listening closely to hear what gift Coach Brickman had chosen for the Good Girl.

"I don't think this is your year, Erin," he said, adjusting his white visor. Beads of sweat had gathered just under the rim, which had begun to discolor with age and weather and dirt, like pink mold around a bathroom sink. "We got a solid team. These girls have been playing together for years. There isn't room for a project. We gotta get to State, you know? If you wanna play next year, spend the winter working on your game. We'll go from there?"

I nodded only, my face reddening quickly, and I gathered my racket, water bottle, and the new duffel bag my mother had purchased

A SHORT LIST OF CHILDHOOD ACCOLADES

001. Varsity Swim Team Captain / MVP
002. Honor Roll
003. Student Council
004. Dance Team
005. Key Club
006. Snoball Queen
007. Drama Club
008. Speech Team
009. Show Choir
010. Spelling Bee Winner

YOUR TURN?

_____
_____
_____
_____
_____
_____
_____
_____
_____

for me. "Erin's playing tennis now," she had said into the phone just the night prior. "I know! I know! It really is something. Just one week in."

The "solid team" stood motionless as their eyes followed me off the court, surprised by his decision. No one, it seemed, had ever been cut from the tennis team. And if ever there had been, it wouldn't be the girl who had spent a lifetime amassing achievements that dotted the school's bulletin board like confetti on a cake.

I waited for practice to end and fought back tears on my silent ride home. My neighbor didn't say anything as she raced through our neighborhood. We both knew there were no more tennis stories to share.

I cried the moment I made it inside my front door, and then I fell onto my bed in a heap of hormones and inadequacy. I later learned that my mother called the tennis coach that evening, asking if I could shadow the girls during practice to learn some pointers for next year.

It was no use. I had chosen tennis, and it hadn't chosen me. I had become a jester on the court, and I wanted to be queen.

There are two reactions to failure. Some people see it as a valuable experience, an opportunity for learning, a road to growth.

And some people see it as a zero on their scorecard, a red letter on their chest, a crayon mark through the second verse of "Amazing Grace." They see it as a flaw in their personality that cannot be changed but can be hidden.

At school the following Monday, news had spread. "I hadn't liked the sport much anyway," I explained with a shrug. "Besides, I have a triathlon in June. I don't need the distraction."

I later won the triathlon for my swim team's age group. I became queen again, in my mind only, of course, and the reign taught a valuable lesson that dictated my behavior for the next decade: all failures can be forgotten if we (a) ignore them, (b) spin them, and (c) pretend they were the plan all along.

Do you know how to spot a forced smile? It's in the irises. If they don't reflect light, even a hint of glow, you might be looking at a happiness fraud.

"Are you ever afraid of Ken dying? Of the tumor winning?" my new boss asks over a lukewarm cup of Peet's Coffee on the Manhattan Beach pier. Ken and I have just moved to the south bay and landed dream jobs: mine in an ad agency; Ken's in a film-trailer editing studio. As we sip our Sumatras, dog walkers whiz by on rollerblades and kids fight the wind to untangle kite strings, catching sand in their eyes.

"Not really," I say, wiping the smudges from my sunglasses with my dress hem. "Who's to say I won't go first? I mean, we could all get hit by a train at any minute, right?"

By now, this is an automatic response. I tell myself this weekly, daily. Is it denial or faith or logic or some fusion cocktail of them all? Maybe it depends on the day.

"Look around," she says. "Do you see any trains?" Nearby, a skateboarder flings himself over the handrail and crashes to the ground, causing a series of thuds. His friends laugh as he pulls himself up with a skinned knee, and they continue down their own personal concrete highway.

Only the ones in my head, I think, as I pitch the coffee in the trash. It has grown cold.

Ken's tumor is the one circumstance I will never be able to manipulate. I was alone, and then he came along with this love, and with this love came a tumor. And I cannot brush that aside with an excuse. I cannot distract myself with a triathlon. I cannot solve it like a mathematical equation; the variables are not in my favor.

I cannot pretend I might be happy with this outcome.

And while I am telling myself to be content hour by hour with this man I love and chose for as long as we both shall live, I am not content.

The lion roars. It wants so much more. It wants mathematical certainty. Control. Absolutes and always.

And I do too.

We are meant to keep an eye on it.

THE LION ROARS. IT WANTS SO MUCH MORE.
IT WANTS MATHEMATICAL CERTAINTY. CONTROL.
ABSOLUTES AND ALWAYS.

3.

TWELVE, WHEN ROUNDED UP?

All human plans [are] subject to ruthless revision by Nature, or Fate,
or whatever one preferred to call the powers behind the Universe.
—*Arthur C. Clarke*

It is an odd thing to have a panic attack when nothing, truly, is wrong.

At the time, I didn't know there was a name for general, underlying anxiety. I knew only that when it rose to the surface, it was very much like suffocating, oxygenless, in one of those children's ball pits as I struggled to find up and out. I knew only the feeling of plastic balls and sneakered feet pummeling me from all directions.

The first, then. Years ago, in college. I am in my apartment kitchen, with its midwestern oak cabinetry and gold knobs that have been tarnished by hundreds of coed thumbs rummaging at 3:00 a.m. for Lucky Charms and bagels and a roadmap for life.

Will I know it when I see it?

It is in this kitchen that I have spilled rice after a particularly taxing day of exams. I have been missing Ken, who is in Los Angeles interviewing for whatever one interviews for when one is a teenage film prodigy. The story has grown old. He is there, I am here, he is here, but not really here, and I am feeling overwhelmed with heavy textbooks, with final projects, with an internship that will begin in a week, and I haven't the faintest idea what I am to be doing—with my internship or with my life.

I want answers, and they are not in the oak cabinets.

One study reports a median survival rate of 11.6 years; another reports a median survival rate of 16.7 years.

Which will it be? Eleven? Twelve, when rounded up? Or will it be seventeen? The time it takes to raise a child? The time it takes to build a life together, a life that seems to begin with an ending?

The rice bag spills, that is all, but the grains fall to the floor and so do I. And I cannot pick either of us up. It is all too heavy, the rice and the missing and me, and I have forgotten everything else about that moment except for the tears and the phone and Ken's voice saying that I don't have to go to the

A FEW PLACES WHERE I HAVE HAD PANIC ATTACKS

001. At Bed, Bath and Beyond, comparing towel prices.

002. In the university library, after receiving a late fee for a transcription machine I could not remember ever borrowing. (I hadn't; it was a mistake, and still, the panic attack.)

003. On my wedding day, after the soccer game. I didn't have anything borrowed. I didn't have anything blue.

004. In an airplane bathroom somewhere over Idaho, somewhere over the cloud carpet. Life felt small, life felt big. There were no paper towels.

005. At a Dave Matthews Band concert. He had sung "Grey Street," that's all.

006. Backstage before keynoting a global conference via telecast. I was supposed to talk about being a big fish in a bigger pond, but really, I just wanted to ask if everyone else was drowning too.

007. In a Japanese restaurant, table for two. There was loud chewing, flame crackling, sake toasting. It had felt dark. Nothing was wrong, except for all of it.

008. While babysitting my nephew. The responsibility had felt heavy, weighty, suffocating. We were playing Chinese checkers and I couldn't find one of the marbles. Should I google "how to give the Heimlich to a three-year-old"? Should I ask him if he swallowed it? But if he didn't, I surely didn't want to give him any ideas. It was blue, the missing marble.

doctor, but I do need to put on pants and shoes, and then we will talk about the doctor.

It's a bright, sunny day and of course everything is fine. No one is dying, for now. *We are meant to keep an eye on it.* This is not yet the end of the world. A few exams and a long-distance relationship and the rice shouldn't be weighty enough to tip the scale, should they?

And so there is guilt braided into the anxiety. It is a rope, a noose, because you have a warm bed and a well-stocked pantry and look, you have found love, and would you just get up off the floor already? Put on your pants and pull yourself together.

When you're raised in the church, it is likely your faith will manifest itself on a souvenir shelf. You gather memorabilia from vacation Bible school plays and summer camps and Christian rock concerts, WWJD bracelets, favorite verses that were taped to your lockers, missionary prayer cards held tight under magnets on your parents' refrigerator. And you look at them, on particularly dark nights, and you think, Ah, yes, here I am. Here is the shelf of a Christian. Here is what this all should look like. Here are the artifacts that point to God. Surely I am on the right track.

And this is where I am on the day of the

panic attack, in the rented kitchen, over the spilled rice. I am surveying my souvenirs, and they are in need of dusting.

T'was Grace that taught my heart to fear.

Will my souvenirs be enough? Can they be? If I obtain another, will my shelf carry the weight? Will I see past the dust? Maybe if I add just one more thing, here, just to the left . . .

Again I hear the lion's roar for more.

It's just that I have been working so hard. I have been working to be perfect. I have been working to please God, and God's people, and to be a better woman with better abs.

Will I know it when I see it?

I am tired, that is all.

The panic attacks made no sense. They approached in wild waves, rhythmic and anticipated and ill-timed, like at the grocery next to a perfect mound of pink apples or in the shower. I cried and cried, and when they passed, I wrote.

I keep a few of those writings on an old flash drive in my office now, nestled on a shelf between expired contracts and Christmas forever stamps. I pull them out from time to time, just to see, just to remember. When I do, I read the words of a young girl who kept working so hard for more, even when it was making her so much less.

4. THE WATER IS HERE FOR YOU

*I suspect that the mind, like the feet, works at about three miles an hour. If this is so,
the modern life is moving faster than the speed of thought, or thoughtfulness.*
—*Rebecca Solnit,* Wanderlust

Ken and I slowly settle into Los Angeles, and my anxiety, my pushing, my attempts at perfection subside for a bit. There is a new apartment to distract myself with decorating—Sunny Side Up for the kitchen, Lady Luck in the bedroom?—and we're just a few blocks from the ocean, and hey, it's Friday night, how about chips and salsa on the pier?

It is blissful, for a few months, in a blissfully boring way. The dented copper measuring spoons for Saturday morning pancakes, the poorly tuned piano that still holds a masking-tape mark on middle C.

While friends our age visit cultural events, go to concerts, and throw dinner parties with fancy cheese, we unpack our old Nintendo and battle our best friend Trav in Super Mario Brothers 3. For two kids who grew up in suburbia, home is simply a place to reheat pizza rolls and ignore the laundry. There is little to be said for museums.

It is sunny in November, a novelty I think I'll never tire of, and we are mostly happy. But on weekends, our families call with tales of first snows and ice skating, and I dig my toes further into the sand, trying to find that first layer of chilled earth, of dampened comfort.

When I finally do visit a doctor to make sense of my sadness, of the anxiety, of the panic attacks that interrupt our weeks, he looks at me incredulously.

"You have graduated, transplanted across the country, married, and started a new job all in the span of a few months? You think your husband will die within ten years? You certainly should be having panic attacks."

He gives me a sheet from his Rx pad—a prescription for an antidepressant—with a note scrawled on the back. "Just breathe," it says.

What am I looking for?

I walk to the parking lot, feeling deflated. A pill and a breath, he says. Surely this is not the answer. Surely there must be more.

Will I know it when I see it?

I pull on my shades, although I don't need to. There are clouds in my eyes.

Later, I meet a coworker for a surfing lesson on the foamy shores of Manhattan Beach. Although I am a swimmer at my core—I have competed in hundreds of races since childhood—never have I surfed. There is no surfing in Indiana, and so I bought a used wetsuit and borrowed a surfboard and we waddled into the sun while the tide was high.

We go through the basics on the sand: footing, paddling, "popping up"— the term for standing on your board as you catch a wave. She tells me the biggest rookie mistake is when beginners pop up on their knees instead of their feet. They kneel instead of squat.

"It seems easier to kneel, but it's not," she says. "It's too hard to pull yourself up once you're there. Just go for it. All in, you know? Surfing isn't a halfway thing."

We move from the sand to the water, and as we paddle out to catch our first wave, I instinctively know that I am terrible at surfing. I try the pop-up, but I fail and flail and I surface each time with a bruised spirit and sandy teeth. Once, I think I have caught a wave and force myself up too early. My board flips from under me and I crash into the ocean floor, hard. I am stunned and disoriented.

It is enough to make me run (waddle) away from surfing entirely. But my coworker says something good to me, something I still remember because I wrote it down that day. It had seemed worth writing down, I suppose, and it is now on the flash drive, waiting between the Christmas stamps and the contracts.

"Stop relying on your strength," she says. "The water is here for you. It's stronger than you are. Let it do the work. Try again this time with less you and more water."

I listen and nod and return to my board in my shiny penguin suit, buoyed by my coworker's great surfing advice. I want to make excuses for myself—my hair is growing heavy with seaweed, there is sand in my eye—but I fight the urge. I am growing up, it seems, right here in the Pacific Ocean. Do you see? Can you see me rising?

I paddle and wait, I pop up and crash, and I do this a few more times, but then I do not. A wave comes to me, and it carries me, and then I am above it, onto it, on the cusp of something heavy and light and deep and wide, and I am crouching, then standing, then riding to shore.

Stop relying on your strength. The water is here for you.

In my mind's ocean are jaws of depression, tentacles of anxiety. I live daily in the hope that if I work hard enough, if I paddle

SUMMER '06

fast enough, I might outswim the sadness. I might outsmart the tension. I might overcome life's ambiguity with sheer will, force of mind.

Surely I am strong enough to overcome it all?

Try again this time with less you and more water.

"But whoever drinks the water I give them will never thirst. Indeed, the water I give them will become in them a spring of water welling up to eternal life" (John 4:14).

I remember this verse from my childhood. I have read of this concept in my parents' church with the dusty red hymnals, the wedding, the stone altar.

I don't mean to imply that depression can be cured only by God, with a few empty prayers and a worship song. I don't believe this. But I do know that with God come wisdom and time, and with wisdom and time comes perspective, and that sometimes, overcoming depression requires an oversized cocktail shaker of all of those things, on the rocks, please.

My coworker and I drag our boards to the shore, muscles exhausted and minds clear. We brush the sand off our feet and squeeze wet toes into our sandals, and she asks me how I like surfing so far.

I take mental stock. I am feeling light. I am feeling strong. I am feeling . . . happy?

"I don't know," I say. "It seems kind of hard."

I do the work. I take the pills. I read the books. I do the breathing exercises.

We were meant to keep an eye on it.

I visit an energy therapist in Santa Monica who commands that I stand on one leg for thirty minutes, and on the other for another thirty. We are standing there, flamingos, silent in a tiny room smelling of incense and old carpet. There are no windows. There are no coffee tables, no sofas, no brochures with stock photos of a woman in a button-down shirt in a cubicle, caressing her furrowed brow under a boldface header: "Could you be depressed?"

When our session is over, when I am told to cease the flamingo position, the energy therapist smiles and says, "Well, I'll see you next week."

"Next week?" I ask.

"You are very imbalanced."

Every day, I commute to my desk job in Beverly Hills. My official title is Executive Assistant at one of the most successful concert production companies in the world, but my job responsibilities are filing invoices, offering green tea refills to visiting musicians, and once or twice taking celebrities' dogs out for a poop.

I watch the clock and daydream away the hours, feeling the weight of what I fear is the beginning of a wasted life. I have been taught in church that God has a very specific calling for me—just me!—and surely it doesn't involve monitoring the bowel movements of a celebrity's favored companion.

It seems irreverent to waste a full life, if that is indeed what I've been granted, in a job I know holds little purpose for me. What about Ken? What about his elevenish years? Or will it be 16.7? How can I mindlessly whittle away my days when so few are offered to him?

But sometimes, often, the most reverent spiritual practice is to pick up the pug dung and get back to work.

Try again this time . . .

On my drives home from the office, I listen to Louise Hay and Lucinda Bassett CDs. I repeat calming affirmations as BMWs and Vespa drivers without helmets zip past me—*I am in complete control over my reactions*—and I begin to learn the importance of acceptance, of living in the present tense. I begin to learn to allow things to happen as they are, rather than how I want them to be. I begin to learn, quite simply, the art of peace.

Peace is a lofty word with spiritual implications. It can mean a great many things, but sometimes peace simply means that when the barista at Noah's Bagels gives you the wrong cookie—you'd ordered macadamia nut, and isn't this chocolate chip?—and you don't notice until you're back on the freeway, you eat it and smile and go on with your day. (It tastes like your grandmother's recipe. Have you ever noticed that?)

Once, at work, I pass a woman from HR who is smoking a cigarette in the breezeway by the Keurig machine. "I cannot do this one more day," she says to me.

I shift my folders to the other hand and glance at my watch. I have three minutes before the next meeting, something involving Coldplay's next show. "What's up?" I ask.

"This job. It's sucking the life out of me," she says between drags. "Literally, sucking it. Do you know I used to be a ballerina?"

I study her, and I believe it. Her face looks sullen, ashy, but I can see there's a mix of strength and softness about her. "Do you still dance?"

"Only over my own grave," she says, putting out her cigarette stub in a pod of green tea. I watch her expensive heels *click-clack-click-clack* into the meeting, and I wonder how many of us are trading in our peace, our passions, our pliés in search of something more. How many of us are fighting for the American dream, running the rat race, praying to scale Maslow's self-actualization pyramid, when really we just want to dance?

. . . with less you and more water.

Maybe there's a little bit of pug dung on everyone's ballet slippers.

BUT SOMETIMES, OFTEN, THE MOST REVERENT SPIRITUAL PRACTICE IS TO PICK UP THE PUG DUNG AND GET BACK TO WORK.

5.

ON THE HUNT

It takes a level of creative depression to hear
"Girls Just Wanna Have Fun" and weep.
—Sloane Crosley

There is a video of me as a child—five years old, maybe six?—on Easter. My mother has hidden eggs throughout the back yard, small bits of plastic confetti hiding among weeds and dandelions and long blades of grass. I want them all. I want them a whole, whole lot.

As the youngest, I am given an advantage. I am allowed to set out on my gathering mission first, before the older kids can fill their baskets. Youngest to oldest, as the rule goes.

I begin gingerly, taking my time. The grass is mine. I am master of the domain. I choose a pink egg, an orange one, an oversized mint-colored one that might be hiding a chocolate bunny. And I *love* the chocolate bunnies. But then my kingdom is overrun by another child—my older cousin. Soon afterward, my older sister. And another and another, and my perfect nation of civilized candy gathering has gone topsy-turvy.

The older girls whoosh as the wind catches their tangled blonde locks, and I glance down at my basket—three eggs. I have only three eggs.

I look around me as my sisters and cousins scoop eggs by the handful—running, yelping, amassing seven, eight, nine eggs each—and I start to run, but I cannot catch up.

And so I do what the youngest child of three does. I pretend to fall down, I pretend I have spilled all of my eggs and cannot retrieve them, and I manufacture my tears.

Here are things you can think of, as a five-year-old, that might conjure tears: *Life is not fair. Everyone is better than me. I am giving up. More eggs.*

Here are things you can think of, as a twentysomething, that might conjure tears: *Life is not fair. Everyone is better than me. I am giving up. More mascara, then.*

Likely you can imagine the end of this story. I am scooped up by a well-meaning adult who trusts far too much in the emotional stability of a young child, and a new Easter tradition is born:

All eggs will be collected at the end of the hunt and distributed equally among all participants.

I was proud of my antics. They worked, and I kept them in my back pocket for years.

But I am not proud of them now.

Here I am, a new career woman, with Easter eggs that have higher-stakes contents—work, relationships, fulfillment, finances, opportunity, creativity—and one day, in an officewide memo about downsizing, I lose my job. I am to pack my things and go home.

Stunned, I have lost my basket, and my mother is not here to divide the eggs equally.

What to make of this? What to make of the gifts we have been given, of the gifts we wish we had? Of the glittery pink Easter egg glimmering in the sun, the one that almost certainly contains a coveted prize, the one your cousin swiped just moments ago?

We have been taught that we can do anything we set our minds to. We can conquer all! The world is our oyster!

"Do you think the wren ever dreams of a better house?" Poet Mary Oliver wrote this.

But when we cannot conquer all, when we cannot have our way, it is easy to blame our circumstances, to point to our barren oyster and lament what little it holds. Who wants to admit that, today, we cannot produce a pearl for reasons we don't yet understand?

Not me.

"Can I get you anything?" Ken asks.

"No thanks," I say.

It is Friday night, and the cardboard box containing things from my office—my (largely blank) day planner, vanilla hand sanitizer, the miniature penguin ornament from my Secret Santa, and a stack of neapolitan Post-its I'd pilfered before leaving the building—is scattered flippantly on the kitchen counter.

"How about takeout? Chinese?" he asks.

"I'm going to go lay down," I say.

I am already lying on the couch, but retreating to the bed seems a more fitting idea. The couch is where Ken is, and he knows nothing of empty oysters. Just last week, he received a promotion in Hollywood—a dream gig for his age—and he is, at this moment, swimming in pearls. We had celebrated on the pier over mojitos and key lime pie. A toast to our bright futures in editing bays (him) and dog excrement (me).

The only thing worse than allowing yourself to be a victim is to resent the survivors. To wish that sometime, in the middle of the night, a robber might come and steal everyone else's pearls too.

But hadn't I wanted to slow down? Hadn't I secretly wanted this, a break from the mundane, the purposeless? An escape hatch from the car barreling too fast down a road I hadn't intended to travel?

A lion knows nothing of what he wants. He only fills the hunger inside. And when he's emptied, when you take away his kill, the leftover scraps, the unloved pieces, he is angered by the loss.

And on he prowls.

I spent the next few years changing jobs, switching careers, seeking fulfillment.

There were afternoons spent taking personality tests, reading business books borrowed from the library. On breaks from temp jobs, I submitted writing samples to my favorite magazines in the hope of penning a freelance article on style, on substance, on anything at all.

Sometimes Ken would come home from work late to find me in bed, curtains drawn, my cold breakfast cereal on the nightstand, dog-earing pages of *What Color Is Your Parachute?*

"How long have you been in here?" he'd ask, knowing the answer was all day, knowing the answer was I haven't yet moved, knowing the answer was I'm not leaving here—not this apartment, not this room, not this bed—until I figure out what to do with my life.

On a good weekend, I'd shut the books

and open the laptop and write what I thought to be beautifully witty articles, but then I'd read *McSweeney's* in the afternoon—"What the Corinthians Wrote Back to the Apostle Paul"; "Bedtime Stories by Thom Yorke"— and delete everything in a rush of inadequacy.

Once, I called my friend Lisa, a social worker in Indiana, asking her how she knew what she wanted to do with the rest of her life. She told me stories of foster home visits and juvenile detention ministries and broken families and how it had just seemed like she could do something—anything—about one small part of it.

"It's like that saying," she said. "Sometimes it's more important to be useful than to be happy."

Ralph Waldo Emerson. That's who said it:

"The purpose of life is not to be happy. It is to be useful, to be honorable, to be compassionate, to have it make some difference that you have lived and lived well."

But I was still operating with the mentality that to be useful, I had to *feel* useful. I hadn't yet learned that sometimes the being comes before the feeling.

Ken used to talk about this. He often gave pragmatic answers for the reasons he chose to do things—the reason he chose to move to Hollywood within two years of his diagnosis, the reason he became a film editor, the reason he married me.

"It seemed better than the alternative," he said.

We didn't talk about which alternative he meant.

A median survival rate of 11.6 years; another of 16.7 years.

In my endless search for meaning, I bought the lie that work—a title, a calling card, a byline, a corner office—offered usefulness. Purpose. A way to make a difference.

But of course, what we do is not who we are, and although we know this, we still, continually, over red-pepper bisque at a dinner party, ask each other what we do for a living.

I wanted a good answer to this question. I wanted not to say *umm* before giving my response.

When I did have a good answer, a great job, when I did not need to say *umm*, it was still, of course, not enough. A bad day at the office could render me useless, horizontal on the sofa, eating blue fish gummies and mourning my lack of luck. I vacillated between complaining about others and complaining about myself, feeling convinced

This is a superbly nutritious vegan version, known to satisfy even the pickiest of soup slurpers.

Ingredients

3 small red bell peppers, chopped

1 carrot, chopped

1 small yellow onion, chopped

1/4 cup raw cashews

1/2 cup vegetable broth

1 clove garlic, peeled

2 Tbsp red wine vinegar

1/4 cup coconut milk

Pinch of sea salt

Pinch of black pepper

001. Throw everything in a blender and blend on high for about a minute (or on a soup setting, if you've got it). Done and done.

002. For optional, additional effort: top with a sprinkle of oregano and avocado slices.

that I'd be the woman I wanted to be if only my circumstances would change. When they did change, I felt happy. When they didn't, I felt defeated.

Do you know what happens when we victimize ourselves? When we hand over our power to circumstances? We lose everything that matters. We lose the freedom to change, the grace to rise above, the strength to get up off the couch.

We have given the power away. We can no longer conjure it when we need it most.

And let's be clear: we will need it most.

Every now and then, I'd find tiny moments of joy—a picnic in the park with new acquaintances or a leisurely stroll through the mall. Family would visit and we'd eat shrimp pasta from boats docked on the pier. We washed our whites. We checked the mail. Life went on.

Once, Ken's mother flew into town and bought bubbles at the drugstore. We blew them in the living room, dripping soap onto the rugs, the sofas, the throw pillows, and we watched our dog, Bernie, bark frenetically and gobble each and every sphere. I laughed like the sadness would never return. That was one of the good days.

But a lot of times it felt like life wasn't happening around me or with me, but rather was happening *to me*. It felt like life was something to figure out (should I take Sepulveda Boulevard or the 405?), an enigma to be solved (maybe if I wake up an hour earlier . . .), but the cards were simply not being dealt in my favor (16.7? That's it?).

I later learned that thinking about living is not the same as living.

It was perhaps a classic case of being a young gal with far too much time on her hands, with far too many thoughts swirling about, with far too much selfishness at her disposal.

What am I looking for?

Bernie used to eat puzzles. Ken and I would spend a Sunday evening on our balcony

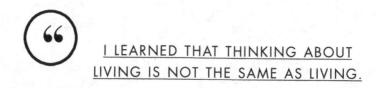

I LEARNED THAT THINKING ABOUT LIVING IS NOT THE SAME AS LIVING.

overlooking an indigo ocean, chatting as we put together a jigsaw of a thousand pieces. We'd find the corners, the edges, the picture would begin to form, and hours later, we'd have finished a bottle of wine only to find that the puzzle would never be revealed, at least not in its entirety.

There were seventeen missing shapes, and Bernie had a stomachache.

I suppose I thought life was the puzzle. That it was meant to be lived, to be understood, to be unriddled with the help of the ocean and a bottle of wine.

But the puzzle isn't life, is it? The ocean, the wine, the Sunday evening on the balcony—that's life. It's enough to be enjoyed, with or without the missing pieces.

Once I learned this—once I stopped questioning the empty puzzle spaces—the panic attacks began to slow.

Eventually, we switched to checkers. Far better for the dog's health.

00

6.

A VERY AMBITIOUS DOMAIN NAME

I'd finally come to understand what it had been:
a yearning for a way out, when actually what
I had wanted to find was a way in.
—*Cheryl Strayed*

What do you do for a living, Erin? Umm . . .

My response to this dinner party question is always at least three sentences.

"Well, there's the local boutique ad agency where I sometimes spend my days copywriting ("Like patents?" they ask. "Like marketing brochures," I say), but mostly I can be found washing my boss's boyfriend's BMW or delivering Napa merlot to clients. Oh! And I've sold my first freelance article . . ."

My voice trails off at the same time as their interest.

Ken, with his one-word response— "filmmaker"—is due for another promotion. His work has earned him industry accolades and growing respect within the company. His health is stable, and as a young wife to a man with an expiration date, that is certainly all I can ask for.

But really, I want a house.

Of course, it isn't a house that I want. It is security, stability, a guarantee that this wild life can be controlled, understood, tidied, and surely I can face anything with a brick townhome and a side yard, and a washer and dryer, please.

(Plus a wooden fence, the perfect puzzle border from which to fill in the blanks.)

But life doesn't offer security, and so, I choose a house instead. It comes with a rickety side porch swing that I despise from the beginning—faded hunter green with thick ticking stripes—and I promise myself we'll replace it immediately.

Did you catch that? I wanted to replace a porch swing, a symbol of peace and contentment, of hearth and home, of family and memories, because I did not like the color, the pattern, the rust. It was not beautiful enough. It was not what I had envisioned.

The year is 2006. The weather, daily, is sunny and seventy.

Likely I do not have to tell you how easy it is for the bright-eyed young couple in Los Angeles to waltz into any bank and get a loan. *Stated income? Pinky swear? Sign by the X. Here are your keys. Congratulations and best wishes! Enjoy this complimentary doormat. It's on us.*

We later find out that from the west coast to the east, from the skyscrapers to the silos, loans and doormats are being doled out to anyone and everyone, free popsicles on a school field day.

But the free popsicle is not free.

The house—stucco, beige, traditionally traditional—has the look of a sleeping giant's face if you see it from the front, from across the street. There are two windows (eyes) framed atop a centered balcony (nose), and when the garage door opens, the giant yawns slowly until the car is parked, then shuts his mouth to continue his nap, swallowing all inside.

It's funny; you write things down in black and white, and there are facts that turn red the instant they arrive on the screen. Our house in Los Angeles, the price, the loans, the debt. They are all red now.

There are the things you see, and then there are the other things.

For two years, we rent out the first floor of our townhome to acquaintances while we live on the main floor above, faithfully pooling our dollars to pay a monthly mortgage that costs more than a year's rent in Indiana.

Our home becomes the scene for a quirky rotating cast of characters. Renters come and go, bringing with them a slew of inconveniences from yipping Chihauhaus to marijuana habits. Once, a tenant's girlfriend spends the night downstairs, and the next morning Bernie steals her underwear while she is in the shower.

"Erin." Ken calls me at work, whispering. "Bernie just came into my room with a black lacy thing from downstairs. What do I do? Do I knock on the bathroom door to return it? Is that weird? I don't even know her name! Do you think she wants it back?"

We are young and a little bit dumb. Mostly, we are just young enough to think we aren't dumb at all.

At my wedding shower years ago, I sat in the middle of a circle in a tiled church fellowship hall to receive the wisdom of aunts, mothers, grandmothers, sisters, and cousins who had learned the art of marriage. Between plastic forkfuls of white sheet cake, the advice rang in:

"Always keep something lacy in your underwear drawer!"

"Never go to bed angry with one another."

"Store two lasagnas in the freezer—one for births, another for funerals."

And there was this piece of advice that I thought of often, that I still think of often, when I'm drying the dishes and preheating the oven and scrubbing bacon grease off the backsplash:

"Don't worry about matching your jewelry to your shoes or your handbag. Match it to the kitchen sink. That's where it'll end up anyway."

My wedding ring, a thick stainless band, matched our dark granite countertops *perfectly*. I noticed this the week we moved in.

There it sat, glistening in our new kitchen, the one just for us, for us and the renters, for us and the renters and the dogs and our happiness.

MY FAVORITE STYLING (AND LIFE?) TRICKS

001. When in doubt, add a plant. A rubber plant is foolproof to start with—nearly impossible to kill—and it's known to clear the air of formaldehydes, chemicals, harmful vapors. You'll have to clear the rest of the toxins (bitterness, regret, discontent) yourself, but a kickstart helps. No one ever said no to a little helping hand from nature.

002. Edit, edit, edit! Say no to the newest dish towel pattern. Resist another limited-edition hand-poured balsamic cedar soy candle. Practice self-control in the stationery aisle at Target, even when the floral envelopes are on sale. (And don't you dare buy another book about decluttering.) There is much value in self-control.

003. There is very little that cannot be solved with a good scrubbing and a fresh coat of paint.

I prefer a hot soak with a good scrub, but everyone's got their thing.

004. Scoot your furniture into the center of the room and anchor it with a rug. Living rooms are for living, for gathering, for having conversations with each other. It is nearly impossible to do this when up against a wall. This is true in most scenarios.

005. You can never have too much natural light. Open the curtains, the blinds, the windows. Let in the sun, let in the clouds, let in the moonlight. Sheers are best for this, even in the bedroom. If you can't walk around in your undies at home without worrying about how much the neighbors can see, you can either (a) move to the country or (b) stop worrying about how much the neighbors can see.

A new mortgage meant a new job, and I began picking up styling work in addition to my ad agency job.

What do you do for a living, Erin?

Umm . . .

My dinner party response grew far beyond three paragraphs.

I want to tell you, briefly, the difference between a stylist and an interior designer.

Both work in the business of upgrading, making new, reinventing, repurposing. Before to after. Old to new. Ugly to not ugly, in a matter of personal opinion.

They do this, of course, in very different ways. You'll invite an interior designer into your home, and she'll drop her Clare Vivier clutch onto the entryway table and pull out a tape measure as she calls her construction

006. A place for everything, and everything in its place. Your place doesn't have to be everyone's place, by the way. My friend stores her purse in the microwave. She has never, not ever, not once, had to ask anyone where she left her purse.

007. Stick to one color scheme, then allow yourself to experiment within the constraints. Play with pattern, texture, scale, and shade, as long as you're sticking to your color scheme. Enforce boundaries, not rules. (This works for parenting as well.)

008. Art can be found anywhere, in anything. Frame your dad's bomber jacket. Hang a collection of cutting boards from your grandmother's farm. Spend the afternoon chewing gum with a girlfriend and make weird sculptures with spare toothpicks. If it makes your heart sing, it's art.

009. Alternately, if that popular lomography print of the gelato seen in every home tour online doesn't make your heart sing, it's not art.

010. If it does not add value, it does not add much.

011. If it does not add meaning, it does not add much.

012. If it does not add purpose, it does not add much.

YOUR FAVORITE IDEAS HERE:

_____

_____

_____

_____

_____

guy—interior designers *always* have a guy—to ask how soon he can make hickory floorboards happen.

There's not nearly enough light in here. Let's add in a window, south-facing, okay? You've got space for a thirty by sixty, but if we reconfigure the kitchen into a galley—here, let me grab a photo—we could fit a sliding glass door where the fridge used to be. Amazing, right? We'll have to shift the plumbing, of course. And let's go stainless while we're at it. Wait. Fingerprints. Might as well do granite. I'd say marble, but ugh, you cannot even imagine the red wine stains, and you two look like red wine lovers, am I right? What do you think? Want me to run the numbers? Send over a rendering? I can have my guy here next Tuesday to talk flooring.

But if you invite a stylist into your home, she'll begin by taking stock. She will wander, room to room, letting her eyes fall onto your brass table lamp, your antique piano bench, your lace throw pillow. She'll gasp, once or a hundred times at least. She'll gather the hidden gems. She'll ask to see your garage, your attic, your basement. She'll collect, she'll discover, and suddenly she is a flurry of pillow-fluffing, slip-covering, furniture-moving. She'll pull the doilied runner off the Paul McCobb sideboard you tell her you found in your grandfather's shed—*For real?* she'll say as she flips through her paint chip deck. She'll send you to the store with a list—sandpaper, painter's tape, drop-cloth and rollers—and when you return, you'll find your grandmother's handker-chiefs unearthed from the trunk in your bedroom, ironed, perfectly displayed in the mismatched frames that used to hold your doctorate certificates.

A stylist works within constraints, within boundaries. She takes stock, gath-ers, rearranges. She changes very much by changing very little.

And this is why I am a stylist. This is why I begin by taking stock, by gathering, by rearranging. A bit here, a bit there. Quit the gym. Buy a slowcooker.

The alternative is overwhelming to me—drywall dust and new plumbing, and all the guys a renovation requires. I realized that I had been looking at life as an interior designer might look at a project, when really, I was meant to be a stylist.

I was not meant to measure; I was meant to take stock. I was meant to reevaluate, to fluff, to throw a slipcover on the ugly porch swing and call it a life to be enjoyed. I was made for small, for slow, for simple.

"Is there something I can help you find?" the blonde store attendant asks. She is dressed in cowboy boots and a lace skirt with earrings that jingle a bit when she smiles. Her name is Grace.

"Just looking," I say. I'm taking a break from unpacking plates as I walk Bernie through my new neighborhood—a con-glomerate of independent coffee shops, office buildings, thrift stores. Truthfully, an antique purse in the window has caught my eye, but I don't want to spend the money. We still wince as we write our massive mortgage check on the fifth of every month.

I have not yet replaced the porch swing. It hasn't seemed practical.

I walk through aisles displaying boots my grandmother would have worn, and I run my fingers through frilly dresses and polyes-ter prints. It is by far the best vintage shop I've ever seen.

"Are you the owner?" I ask.

"No, I just work here." Grace smiles. "My husband and I are youth pastors."

Ken and I hop into buildings with steeples and sanctuaries every now and then, but we have grown tired of searching for a church with a foil-covered altar where we feel comfortable enough to stick around. At some point, we've stopped trying. At this moment in our faith, church doesn't mean people; it means place.

"You should come," she says. "It's just a few blocks from here. Are you free Sunday night?"

And despite the flashbacks to cold hard pews and camp counselors with not-the-best advice, despite the bad taste that coats my tongue, I hear myself saying, "Yes, I'm free. I'd love to come."

"Is it a casual church?" Ken asks as he pulls a blazer from the closet.

"I don't think it matters?" I say.

Our conversations of late sound like this. Distant, as though we aren't talking about the same thing. I cannot remember when it began, only that it has been months since we've felt light, happy. Ken has been working longer hours to pay the mortgage; I have been not entirely understanding. I have been slowly furnishing the house with thrift finds from my spare styling cash—a fire pit here, a grill there. We'll fix up the exterior first, of course. And we need a sofa soon, and perhaps the matching table lamps from that antique store on Sepulveda Boulevard?

I have not yet mentioned the porch swing. I have not yet mentioned much of anything.

I pull on a white linen shirt and trouser jeans. "Are you ready?"

The church meets in a preschool gym. There is a pile of skateboards to the left of the parking lot, and we enter through double doors to hear a South African accent singing the most incredible, the most swelling, the most hugely moving rendition of "Amazing Grace" we have heard. (There are no hymnals with red crayon marks to mar the second verse.)

The drums slow, the opening prayer is offered. We're late.

Grace sees us approaching the back row and waves us over to two seats she has saved, just left of the middle row. My face reddens, as does Ken's, but when life offers empty chairs, you shuffle over quietly and sit down.

I do not remember the details of the sermon, but by the closing prayer, Ken's hand is in mine, and Grace is smiling, and the incredible, swelling voice is singing again, and we have found, for today, a home away from a house.

Soon Grace becomes Anna and Grace, and then there is Anna and Grace and Jill and Renae, and then it is Anna and Grace and Jill and Renae and Alexis and Heather and Vanessa, and soon enough a friend circle is born. We meet for coffee. We stay late after church. We plan baby showers. We host clothing swaps and dance to Esthero in rooms filled with the smoke of incense. We eat pecan pie with plastic forks on Friendsgiving and dye each other's hair in bathroom sinks with cheap color and foil from the kitchen drawer. We do everything and, in small intervals between, nothing.

My calendar is full of freelance writing assignments and styling jobs, girlfriend get-togethers and church events, and I have little time left for any remnant of sadness, for any stretch of depression. It seems I have two options: chase the busy or chase the blues.

I choose to chase the busy, and so does Ken. He has received another promotion and is clocking roughly sixteen to eighteen hours daily. I go weeks without seeing his face in daylight.

It was the baking sheets that did it.

On a Saturday I don't remember much else of, I was preparing cookies for a tenant's birthday. I preheated the oven, separated the dough, and as I pulled out the baking sheets we had received as a wedding gift just a few short years ago, I saw they had rusted.

I called Ken at work. "Will you be home tonight?" I asked.

"I'm so sorry," he said. "This one's due to the studio by 6:00 a.m."

My new girlfriends were sympathetic to his schedule and often suggested movie night, or dancing? But this night, I didn't want to be cheered. I didn't want to be sympathetic. Instead, I flipped in an old Shins CD and reheated yesterday's pizza and fed the dogs, and I decided to start writing again. I needed a portfolio of my past assignments, and a quiet night in would be good for me.

To the tune of "New Slang," in moccasin slippers and bare legs, I secured the first domain name that popped into my head: Design for Mankind. It occurs to me now that this is a very ambitious domain name. That this is a mark, a mission, a roar from the girl who has finally found something she is good at, something she loves, something whereby she can get to work styling the world, rearranging its mess, and transforming it into something beautiful.

I had blogged before. Years ago, from

a cinderblock dormitory, I spent late nights typing nonsense into a personal Xanga page. Deep, dark secrets from a girl who hadn't yet lived through deep, dark seasons.

But this blog was not that. I was older (not much wiser), more guarded. I was private yet passionate, driven by community and not self. I spent the next ten years and longer typing into this website, sending words into ether, teaching from, talking through. I wrote down many things: art (Klimt! Klee!) and design (Starck! Saarinen!), tales of creative entrepreneurship struggles, plans to pixie cut my hair. I shared links to my freelance articles and created a virtual time capsule of inspirations, a year in review, then two, three, four, and a highlight reel, and I collected words and memories and images as if they were tiny seeds to plant in the fall.

I did not yet realize that, across the world, ordinary people like me were doing the same. Women wearing jasmine perfume wrote in cubicles on their lunch breaks, a stack of take-out menus and kids' doodles in their top desk drawer. Coeds crouched on cheap beanbags in dim dormitories, heads bowed, earphones in, music drowning out their world. Teens sat at oak desks in public libraries surfing the waves of borrowed wi-fi while the eighth graders one table over cheated on their algebra homework. Stay-at-home parents flocked to their computers, having found that, over time, their playgroups were not playful, that the dishwater was dirty, that the hot soapy suds scalded their hands, and that a single LOL comment was just the encouragement they needed to dust-bust yet another Cheerio.

Blogging became our escape, our kingdom, our own personal jungles to rule. Online, we found that, together, if we created enough stories to tell each other, enough stories to tell ourselves, we might finally silence our lions.

And it worked.

Some of us wrote to bemoan porch swings and rusty baking sheets as we searched for churches and missing jigsaw pieces. (We called this finding our voice.) Some wrote to

WE WROTE FOR HAPPINESS, FOR JUSTICE, FOR KNOWLEDGE, FOR PEACE. SOME OF US WROTE FOR SHOES (MYSELF INCLUDED).

create the communities we lacked, posting on forums under surnames and abbreviations. Still others wrote simply to pass the time, penning sweet stories of their kids, sharing advice on sleep training or mountain climbing or financial planning. We were the experts. We were all the experts.

It was a beautiful, momentous time, this era we'd stumbled into in which we became the information we sought. We created the inspiration we so desired.

We wrote for happiness, for justice, for knowledge, for peace. Some of us wrote for shoes (myself included).

Collectively, we began our blogs in a directionless time, and soon our blogs would provide direction. The internet would beckon us, and we would respond in kind.

Few of us anticipated what happened in the next decade—to our internet, to ourselves. Lions are pack animals, after all. The same hunger that seeks community, togetherness, discovery, and expression also roars with pride—with self-doubt, comparison, envy, loneliness. Online, we fed ourselves both.

We feasted on it all.

THINGS I WROTE ABOUT ON MY FIRST BLOG

001. The importance of flesh-colored bandages that coordinate with all skin colors.

002. Top ten most annoying things to ask a college waitress.

003. No, really, please stop asking me if I've had the special. I can afford it only if you tip me seven dollars. But it smells delicious.

004. The beauty of the ninety-nine-cent Ricker's Pop, with strawberry syrup, please.

005. Survey answers, like "Summer or winter?"

006. Pie Day Friday, my roommates' new (ill-advised) tradition in which we feasted on dessert alone for an entire twenty-four hours.

007. A stir-fry "recipe" in which you dip raw broccoli and carrots into a bowl swimming with teriyaki sauce. (This was the first "meal" I prepared for Ken. He was thus unimpressed with my culinary skills.)

008. Snow day football.

009. Everything else.

7.

LORD HAVE MERCY, WE BOWLED

You can't win an argument. You can't because if you lose it,
you lose it; and if you win it, you lose it.
—*Dale Carnegie*

There are two ways to welcome autumn in Los Angeles. The first is to wait patiently and listen, and look outside your front window. If you open it a hair, perhaps half an inch, you'll soon enough notice the tiniest shift in the breeze, a smoke signal that change is on the horizon.

Slowly, the sun starts to set at a lower angle, a few leaves fall, but not many, and the light is so golden, so soft, it feels as if it were never another way. When this particular hue of light arrives, you know it is time to either nap or call your mother.

Pay attention. Wait. Look. Listen. Slow. *What am I looking for?*

There is a second way to welcome autumn in Los Angeles, and that is to make it happen yourself. Force it, and quickly, please. Take a sweater from storage, and maybe a wool hat, and you'll sweat riding your bike to Starbucks for a pumpkin spice latte, but it is October, dang it, and you're feeling festive—let's throw a preholiday dinner party, yes?

You can guess which way I practice.

The dinner party is tomorrow.

*Should I make bacon-wrapped dates? Isn't
Elisabeth a vegetarian? Maybe I'll do those
stuffed mushrooms from Trader Joe's, the fro-
zen ones. Which playlist: John Legend or Ray
LaMontagne? Do we need a warming tray?
Tea lights? I think we're missing a spoon.*

As usual, the things that cause me worry
are not the things that require worrying
about.

After a grocery run—frozen mushrooms
and peonies—I climb the stairs to the kitchen
to see a note on the table: *Went to office. Won't
be long; home for dinner. Love you!*

Once, while dating, Ken and I had dis-
agreed over the difference between *Love you!*
and *I love you.*

"*Love you!* is what you sign in a yearbook," I'd said, and so it had been *I love you*
for us ever since.

But this is how the story goes, isn't it?
It's how so many of our stories go, with or
without the expiration date. Husband wants
to provide for his new wife, to prove his

worth, to show his commitment. New wife
wants to attract her husband's attention and
unwavering focus. To feel her worth, to feel
his commitment. But he is not here. He is
at happy hour—*Wanna come?*—and she is
not—*No thanks*—and she feels replaced,
left behind, forgotten—*Love you!* Tension
builds. Wife grows resentful of his lack of
sensitivity. Husband works more to avoid the
chill in the air. Wife grows resentful of his
absence. Husband works more to avoid the
chill in the air.

Wife grows resentful of the chill in
the air.

And this is where I am, in the kitchen
with the note and the peonies, sweating in
my sweater, resentment oozing from my
pores.

Later, Ken will come home after dinner
to see I have not prepared anything for him.
I haven't yet learned the value of service, of
selfless sacrifice, and am still operating with
a give-and-take mentality. He hasn't earned

dinner, has he? Has he earned much of anything?

He will find me in the master bedroom closet. I will be sitting crosslegged in the corner, having retreated for some space, for some quiet, for some tears. I will have not wanted the tenants downstairs to hear that I am crying, that I have been crying for hours, and I will remember that Ken sometimes uses the master bedroom closet to record voice-overs for clients—it is perfectly sound-deadening—and so, the closet. He will find me there, and it will be silent for a time.

What had our realtor said about this space, this giant, maddening space when we first toured the home? *You could fit an elephant in here.*

You can indeed fit an elephant in here.

We both know we are broken, and we both know we have broken each other.

When someone is shattered, the pieces sometimes break funny, and so we begin to explain in fragments. I am angry. I feel forgotten, left behind, invisible. His career is more important than anything at all—*My career is not more important than anything at all!*—his career, then, is more important than me.

And so it goes: he says something true,

THINGS I SAID

001. I am not happy.
002. I don't want to live here anymore.
003. I hate LA.
004. I hate this house.
005. I hate my job.
006. I hate your job.

THINGS I MEANT

001. Are we going to be okay?
002. Can we survive this?
003. Will you keep me safe?
004. Can you guarantee it?
005. Forever?

she says something imagined, he says something practical, and soon we have forgotten why we are in the closet except to agree on one thing: we have crushed ourselves with an iron fist of unrealistic expectations.

I credit Ken with saving our marriage that night, really, because he said the first kind thing in the middle of unkind things, and that's all it takes. It takes one kind offering. One kind word.

I think what he said was that he wouldn't give up looking for what we'd lost. That we were worth the search.

That we were, after all, meant to keep an eye on it.

We had begun to build something lovely, we decided, and wouldn't it be a shame to sweep the whole thing out with the evening dust?

This is what we'd need to do, of course. We'd need to sweep the whole thing—not the *whole thing*, but the whole thing—out with the evening dust and start anew, to change the story, to fix the ending, to avoid the fate.

If marriage is woven by everyday moments, if the thread that holds together a lifetime of commitment is made up largely of morning breath and lost keys and fingernail clippings and snooze buttons, then truthfully, we'd been unraveling for years.

I couldn't remember the last time I'd kissed his morning breath.

We hadn't paid our dues. We hadn't made the time. We hadn't done the work. Our love had been handed to us, our fate written in the stars, and we thought ourselves defenseless against the sky. Hadn't it been determined years ago? Wasn't it a given? Weren't we promised happily ever after?

But we hadn't earned it. We said yes to marriage, yes to a leap of faith, to a crosscountry move, a star-studded life of Hollywood glitz and glamour. We sealed it all with a kiss, then twirled off and promptly forgot one another, dancing into separate sunsets.

Where was the after in our happily ever?

The thing about the American dream, about marital bliss, about any rewarding pursuit in this world, is this: it isn't a given.

It's a gift.

When you forget this, when you forget to handle this gift with care, you will see that the American dream isn't a dream at all. It is a nightmare, and you have been thrashing through it, your twisted sheets a noose. And you question whether you can live with the snooze button.

THE THING ABOUT THE AMERICAN DREAM,
ABOUT MARITAL BLISS, ABOUT ANY REWARDING
PURSUIT IN THIS WORLD, IS THIS: IT ISN'T
A GIVEN. IT'S A GIFT.

Shortly after the closet, the argument, the elephant, we began thinking. I say that we began thinking not because we were not thinking prior to this, but because it was a different kind of thinking. Our thinking before was like bumpers in a bowling lane—this option or that option, your job or mine, chicken or fish? Either/or.

What am I looking for?

What is said about insanity? It's doing the same thing over and over, expecting different results?

The new way of thinking was, rather, not this or that. It was, simply, must we? Is this essential? Is this imperative? Will this bend us? Will we break?

If forward was wholeness and backward was brokenness, would this decision move us forward? Or send us back from whence we came?

And so we began to remove the bumpers of cultural expectation, and the world became a wildly fun game for two. Sometimes when playing a new game, you make up the rules as you go.

We changed the rules, that is all. The instructions told us that hard work means logging a lot of hours at the office to pay for more things so as to appear you are logging a lot of hours at the office. The instructions told us to work hard, then play hard, but mostly work hard. You can play hard when you're dead. Isn't this called responsibility? Isn't this called wisdom? Straighten up, young man, you've got a mortgage to pay.

We tore the instructions to shreds, and then, Lord have mercy, *we bowled.*

Ken quit Hollywood and began freelancing for film startups and marketing firms. I left the ad agency and filled in the pay gap with income from my blog. I began producing an independent design zine. We visited gallery shows and shopped artist warehouse sales. We went to the pier, over the Ferris

L.A. '07

wheel, to the shore. We held hands in the grocery store. We once ate a pint of ice cream for dinner. For dinner!

It is only practical to use the rooms in our house the way they were intended. The laundry room is for sorting and cleaning. The bathroom is for showering. The living room is for TV watching, or puzzle making, or a Thursday night rousing game of checkers. But what I remember most about this time, this great game without bumpers, is that the rule breaking spilled into our daily lives. We stopped seeing the rooms in our house as having only one specific function or strict purpose, and instead we landed where the moment led us. We ate cold pizza on the living room floor. We had long conversations in the tub. We drank coffee in bed. Once, we slept outside in the side yard in search of stars.

Our life felt slower, lighter, almost instantaneously. We played euchre on the kitchen island; we stayed in our pajamas until noon. I quit my gym. (The irony of sitting in a car to drive to the gym so that I could bike, stationary, fewer miles than I would have gone if I had simply biked to the gym, in the sunshine, with the breeze, was simply too much to bear.) We sold Ken's car and bought a scooter and two helmets. Sometimes we took on odd jobs just for fun. On a slow week in the styling world, I earned $450 walking three beagles around the pier and we bought as many fish tacos as we wanted, saving the rest for a rainy day.

We adopted another dog, George, and soon we were a family of four.

It was not without work. It was not all fun and games. It was not effortless, discarding the rules you'd memorized as a kid. There's a reason those bumpers exist—so our balls don't end up in the gutters.

But Ken and I would never again step back into our life of fast, our Hollywood rat race, our productivity spin cycle. We had come to love our slower life—a life less stressed, less scheduled, less stifling.

For the first time in my life, I was beginning to see the appeal of less.

OO

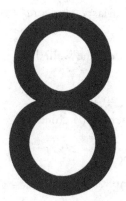

8.
THE VERY WATERS
OF PRODUCTIVITY

Faced with the choice between changing one's mind and proving that
there is no need to do so, almost everyone gets busy on the proof.
—*John Kenneth Galbraith*

After nearly a year of writing daily on my blog, of the styling work, of our slow, small life, my first taste of online success is an email from a popular home-decorating site. "We saw photos of your bedroom," the email reads. "Can we use your space for a feature story?"

"Yes!" I write, but not before I ask how they had come to find my quiet blog. I don't know; I am cautious. My aunt had warned me of internet hoaxes, forever forwarding me mass emails about strange men posing as Tupperware salesmen or, worse, talent agents. "Dear friends of friends," the note would begin. Just last week she had heard of a woman who received a casting call to play the new Rainbow Brite in a community play and was found dead in her apartment hours later, her face painted in a glorious display of Technicolor.

My aunt had said nothing of photo editors for decorating websites, but still, the caution.

"Everyone is reading your blog," the editor writes, and I will tell you this small truth—I am instantly inflated in this moment. Everyone is reading my blog! Everyone is reading my words! I shall send Everyone a thank-you note! I have arrived, I think, as I type my address to the local photographer who is scheduled to come over next Tuesday.

I spend the next few days inside, primping and polishing, vacuuming and varnishing. I rearrange my thrift-store vases roughly thirty-four times, and I spend an inordinate amount of my Saturday afternoon sorting my black paperclips from the white paperclips, carefully funneling them into separate porcelain dishes molded to look like tiny hands. I decant boxes of bowtie pasta, white beans, and linguine into mason jars to display in my kitchen. I reposition my artwork to freshen up the living room, and I re-cover my pillowcases with scarves inherited from my grandmother.

I spend the forthcoming night making our very real home look decidedly unreal, and I do it for the sake of the photos, in the name of inspiration. No, *aspiration*.

(Nothing is to be done with the ugly porch swing. There is only so much I can control; we'll simply have to close the curtains.)

After the photo editor is deemed to be a noncriminal, after the photo shoot wraps,

after the article goes live and is shared by thousands of design enthusiasts, the comments pour in.

"Why are their plates on the wall? Do they eat sideways?"

"Who segregated the paperclips?"

"Someone needs to send this chick to design school."

"Carbs are not decor."

And the capstone, simply, "WTF?"

This acronym I have to look up, and after googling, I stop reading the comments, slam the laptop closed, and boil water for dinner. We will be having pasta.

It wasn't even the comments, the public chastising. It wasn't the brazen opinions of people who despised the lack of color in my home, who thought the living room rug was displaced, who simply could not understand why I would hang porcelain plates as artwork in earthquake country (fair enough, on that one). Those things bothered me, yes, but what bothered me more was that for a brief moment, the week before, I had arrived. Everyone was reading my blog, isn't that what the editor had said? Wasn't I queen?

I wanted the crown without the criticism.

In our great bowling game of bumper-

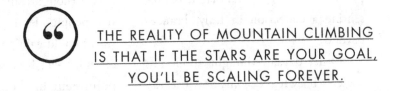

less lanes, of working without expectation, of free-flowing, make-up-your-own-career-as-you-go livelihood, I had landed in the gutter, finally, and it had left me battered, bruised, badly in need of a spitshine.

I wanted my tidy arrival feeling back.

Did you hear the lion rumble just then?

Escaping the concrete jungle of LA and slowing my life had emptied my lion. He was hungry, and he'd moved on to reign over a new wilderness: the internet.

I spent the next few years climbing again, peeking behind me to see how far I'd come and looking ahead to see how much longer it might take.

The reality of mountain climbing is that if the stars are your goal, you'll be scaling forever.

Some days, my intentions were good. I woke up feeling happy and fulfilled. I scrambled the eggs. I thought of the emerging artists who were gaining traction in the art scene because of my blog and other blogs like mine that would soon dictate a new way of being an artist. Upload mixed media graphics today and curate a gallery show tomorrow—isn't that the way it had gone?

Emails arrived thanking me for my contribution to the independent art community. It is an odd thing to contribute something to the world by accident, to know that the rocks, gems, and jewels you collect for yourself have become a mosaic for the world to see, and would you look at how it's shining?

Most days, I took a great deal of pride in the rising popularity of my blog. I found meaning and purpose in spotlighting the beautiful work of others—in the independent jeweler in Portland who gained notoriety from my blog and then used proceeds from her sales to adopt her daughter; in the elementary school teacher whose paintings I promoted and, five years later, is presenting a collection in Italy, France, beyond.

Other days, I thought about my readers. They had become dear friends, in an odd sense of the word, and I thought about Lisa's upcoming gallery show, and Samantha's aging father, and how Pia was doing with her new gig as a waitress in Amsterdam.

But then there were the days that I simply hurried through my work to brainstorm ways to keep myself relevant, better, best. The show must go on, the charade must be maintained. I worked online, and when you work online in a realm where people click links at a frenetic speed, you begin to think of your brain as a pinball machine. You strive to be all things to all people, pinging back and forth like a tiny metal ball until you run out of steam and bounce, bounce, bounce into the chute.

I am not complaining. Pinball can be fun; I liked the sound of it all. *Ping, ping.*

To keep up the pinging, to sustain the momentum, you must say yes to everything you encounter. This seemed easy, I thought, since it fit so well into my people-pleasing tendencies anyway. I could gain popularity and never say no, never have to sense the disappointment in the phone call, never have to conjure another polite way to decline the new media conference in Manhattan.

Weekly, the requests arrived. The internet had opened the thinning clouds of opportunity, and everywhere, thousands of popular bloggers were dancing in the rain, mouths open, eyes to the sky:

"Would you like to curate a collection for our local gallery show?" *Ping.*

"We'd like to partner with you to create a custom line of furniture." *Ping.*

"We're starting a column on young entrepreneurship; are you interested in penning it?" *Ping, ping, ping.*

And so I said yes to it all. I drank of the flood, the very waters of productivity that nearly drowned our marriage years ago.

It took only a short time to discover that success is not a mountain, not a flood, but a mirror. It reflects what the world wants from you, and so you smile and brush the hair out of your eyes, and you play along.

At night, while traveling in the midst of my pinging season, I crawled into crisp white hotel sheets and called Ken to tell him I loved him and was going to bed, and *Yes, yes, all is well here, can you kiss the puppies goodnight for me?* Sometimes before I fell asleep, I wondered if this tiny taste of success was a blessing from God, or a curse that he simply allowed.

It hadn't occurred to me that there was a third possibility, a truer one. That it *was* a blessing from God, but that I had made it into a curse.

00

THE DIRTY SECRET OF MORE

There are two ways to get enough: one is to continue to accumulate more and more. The other is to desire less.
—G. K. Chesterton

Today, I am seated in church. I am distracted, thinking of an upcoming business trip I am taking during which I am to lead a panel about blogging. I have recently been declared an expert in the field, a highly acclaimed resource for writers interested in design or art or living a more beautiful life. The internet said so, so it must be true. The *London Times* said it. *Lucky Magazine* said it. I had not yet said it.

I did not—I do not—think of my life as beautiful. It is just life. And so I worked hard for the charade. I considered the costume.

Should I wear the faux fur vest? Would that be too distracting? Would I spend the day interrupting every introduction with an explanation—*It was my grandmother's! No, really! Don't worry; it's faux.* Should I go with heels or wedges? It's harder to run in heels. Did I have time to get the wedges resoled before Thursday? Could I drop them off after tomorrow's manicure?

I am surveying my cuticles when our pastor, Jon—he is a soft-spoken man in beach sandals, a bit similar to Matthew Perry, perhaps a brother, a distant cousin, a friend?—snaps me back to the sermon, and I hear one line and one line only:

"But woe to you who are rich, for you have already received your comfort" (Luke 6:24).

Yes, it does hurt, this truth. It does hurt very much.

The truth is that blogging has shifted my view. You do not see view shifts until after they have shifted, and so it is only now, only today in church, only after being smacked with a verse from the book of Luke that I notice I am here, surveying my cuticles, my faux, my wedges. My comfort, my prize.

Growing popularity offers more opportunities for products, items, comforts I could never afford before, and I find that the more I receive, the more I say yes—*ping*—the more I am in want. A lion's hunger is insatiable.

Of note: Ken and I do not think ourselves rich. Our mortgage is still outlandishly large, and we consider ourselves, on most days, to be house poor. Only in writing this now do I realize *house poor* to be an oxymoron.

Poor, I thought, was eating Ramen for dinner in a viewless rental without cable. Poor, I thought, was shopping at Goodwill for new shoes.

It was years before I understood the negative effects of my far-reaching consumer-

ism, before I realized that the stick by which I measured wealth and status was heavily skewed. I cannot now conceptualize a more accurate miscalculation of rich and poor. As I am thinking of it, just blocks from this same church, there are groups of children eating ketchup packets for dinner.

I am here, living with one eye on my belongings and another on my soul.

"Would you like to receive our new Espadrille wedges?" yesterday's email read. I would, very much, and I do, very much, and now they are en route to my doorstep, wrapped in tissue with a lovely note of encouragement, of kindness, of praise.

I have no true need for Espadrille wedges. It is a perk, yes, a lovely perk, and yet some perks become so regular, you come to see them as ordinary blessings, and then you come to see those ordinary blessings as daily expectations.

Have I been working for more perks, more accolades, more of the Espadrille wedges, the pink blazers, the conference panels?

Do you know the difference, grammatically, between *more* and *many*? I learned it in college from a professor who had burned her bra in the throes of feminism, who had adopted and raised a thirteen-year-old son alone, who, when her partner had left her for another woman, when she and her son slept on cardboard for a time, had turned to grammar, to education, to self-reliance for her worth.

Many, she explained, is measurable. We owed many large sums of money. We missed many meals. We did not have many items in our care.

And I see it now: the blazer, the manicure. The cappuccino, the conference. The many. Yes, I was measuring it. All the time.

But *more*, she explained, is immeasurable. We wanted more. (How much?) We needed more. (How much?) We would never, ever, I feared, have more. (But how much?)

More, she said, is a never-ending immeasurable. It can't be counted or valued or summed or justified. More is always, by definition, just ahead at the horizon. That's why we never stop chasing it.

More is never enough.

There are two catchphrases I have used, many of us have used, to justify the stress of busy lives spent amassing.

1. God will not give you more than you can handle. (Or the rhyming version: If God brought you to it, he'll bring you through it!)

I think this one to be true. But I also wonder if God has given us a few things—an aging parent, some mouths to feed, a recent job loss—and we have given ourselves many more things—the Target credit card bill, a yard to mow, a bigger house with an extra bedroom for guests, three dinner parties to host, and the inability to say no to serving the animal crackers in Sunday school twice this month. Between God's giving and our own giving, there is excess.

How many, how much?

There are the gifts we thank God for— the opportunity that brings the promotion, the promotion that brings the Target credit card, the Target credit card that brings the new credenza in the new guest room in the

AND I SEE IT NOW: THE BLAZER, THE MANICURE. THE CAPPUCCINO, THE CONFERENCE. THE MANY. YES, I WAS MEASURING IT. ALL THE TIME.

new house with the bigger yard where the flatware will need to be polished before Friday night and *Where'd we leave those peppermint candles?* and *Kids, is that a blueberry on the new white couch?!* and suddenly, we've tipped the scale. We're stressed. We pray for deliverance, for peace, for our joy to return.

We call this a test. Can we handle this? Can we handle the busy? Can we handle a quicker pace, a heftier load?

Perhaps we were never intended to.

God will not give us more than we can handle, the saying goes.

But what does it say about what we give ourselves? What then?

2. God helps those who help themselves.

This one, to be clear, is not in the Bible. Ben Franklin said it, and although I'm grateful for bifocals, Mr. Franklin, I believe this to be ill advice.

I used to hint for gifts from Ken—"How great does this book look?!"—and he would, amazingly, remember the hint, and I would, amazingly, forget the hint, until weeks later, on Christmas or a birthday, I'd unwrap from him the very book I'd impatiently bought myself (and already read). Only his would be inscribed.

Here he was, wanting mostly to give me something lovely and meaningful, and here I was, giving a lesser version to myself because it was immediate. Is it our doing the helping ourselves, and God's wanting to do the helping, but only if we would just get out of the way already? Move over? Quit buying our own books? Stop choosing our gifts based on our own idea of adequate timing?

Oh, but it sounds so tidy. It sounds like if God helps those who help themselves, we get to stomach long hours in cubicles under fluorescent lights; we get to praise the arrival of Monday morning donuts. We get to pack our schedules with another kids' soccer game, another dance lesson, another playdate. We get to check our email under the dinner table. We get to amass money, experience, knowledge. We get to reward our volunteer shift at the homeless shelter with a venti iced mocha latte on the drive home. We get to be the yes-man, the make-it-happen girl, the busy bees. We get to interchange good works with *any* works.

We get to answer *What do you do for a living?* without *umm.* We get to slurp our red-pepper bisques with a smile.

We get to nearly guarantee that this God we believe in, this God who helps those who help themselves, will flood down our due blessings as long as they're earned.

Yes, I'll be on that conference call, in the name of our Lord Jesus, amen.

(Last year, for Christmas, Ken gave me twenty dollars and a smile and told me to go pick out my own book.)

Pastor Jon is offering his closing prayer. I am offering my own.

God, teach me what it means to forgo the riches of this life. Change me. I am spent.

 GOD, TEACH ME WHAT IT MEANS TO FORGO THE RICHES OF THIS LIFE. CHANGE ME. I AM SPENT.

CHASING LESS

10.

We were together. I forget the rest.
—*Walt Whitman*

The cool thing about God, and also the annoying thing about God, is that when he wants to move, he tears down the whole operation, lumbering giant style. Even when he tiptoes, the whole ground shakes.

I'm talking first of the great stock market crash of 2008.

During what economists describe as the worst financial crisis since the Great Depression, many Americans watch Wall Street plummet on TV sets they purchased on credit to furnish living rooms in which they can no longer live.

We are safe, we think. We don't over- extend ourselves; we have the rental income. We have no credit-card debt. We have savings in the bank. We both have steady jobs. We will be fine. We will wait this out.

But it wasn't the plan. It isn't the trajectory we'd considered, and these are not the rules we agreed to.

What is happening was foreseeable to everyone, it seems, except for us. Loans had been doled out, passed around, handed to anyone in the hot summers of 2005, 2006, and beyond by bankers in pinstripe pants. What had my grandmother said? "Never trust a pinstripe pant"?

The realtors had offered clipboards and Montblanc pens—*Sign here! Honestly, folks, it would cost you more money not to buy this house!*—and we'd sent fruit baskets as a thank-you.

We'd assumed our pinstriped loan officer would play by the rules as long as we did. Isn't that how this world works? Doesn't the banker, the realtor, the loan officer praise the good citizen? Doesn't he smile at the compliant child, offer a pat on the head and a warm wink?

Doesn't God?

If you are kind and hardworking, if you pay your taxes and your bills, if you brake for bunnies, won't God bless you?

But we had swum in the ocean amid sharks, had run our sandy feet right past the small and weatherbeaten wood sign: *No lifeguard on duty.* After all, our beach was crowded. No one here seemed worried, and the waves—they beckoned.

And then they crashed.

This hadn't been the plan.
This hadn't been our plan.

I once attended a children's party—a Happy Cinco de Mayo! shindig on April 23rd—proof that in the spring, in the Midwest, after winter has thawed, you're eager to celebrate anything and early. There was cake for the kids, a cheese plate for the adults. Tiny pickles, kalamata olives. When it came time to whack the pinata in the living room, a sixth grader took a bat to the papier-mache donkey and out popped dozens of tiny erasers, confetti streamers, and a handful of multicolored pencils, freshly sharpened. One pencil barely missed puncturing the balloon bouquet; the others fell just short of poking out a sizable number of widened eyes.

My family still jokes about it.

But this isn't funny. Our life is the party, our Los Angeles home is the pinata, and where we expected candy, chocolate, a good outcome, we receive rainbow pencil puncture wounds.

IF YOU ARE KIND AND HARDWORKING, IF YOU PAY YOUR TAXES AND YOUR BILLS, IF YOU BRAKE FOR BUNNIES, WON'T GOD BLESS YOU?

The next few weeks, possibly months, are blurry to me. We wake up, and we shower, and Ken drives to a meeting while listening to the radio DJs talk about the weather—sunny and seventy again—and I bike to the coffee shop on my mint-green cruiser, and we each take a deep breath and go underwater to become productive little submarines—fingers to the keyboard—and when we resurface around 5:00 p.m. or earlier, we remember to worry about things.

At dinner, the reheated kind, I frequently ask Ken how much money we've lost in the home. "Did anything change today? Is the stock market on the up-and-up? Do you have any good news?"

I am not asking Ken. I am asking God.

This is the beginning of my understanding that the home we invested in as our retirement plan, our savings account, our security net will be gone by tomorrow. That the home's value will plummet, that it will lose $200,000 in a single summer, that the pinstriped banker had been wrong, that we will look at the statement, mouths agape, wordless, fearful, directionless.

We had built a house on sinking sand, with cracked plastic shovels and sun in our eyes. And look, just beyond the horizon. The tide's coming in.

It's not going to take much to wash it all away.

We call our lender quickly. The man we speak with is not surprised to hear from us, is not surprised to hear from anyone, and he reassures us that he has a plan, that all will be fine.

"You're gonna want to do a short sale," he says. "I'll walk you through it."

His name is maybe Dan—I don't quite recall—and we have Maybe Dan's direct line, and sometimes a direct line to anyone feels better than a 1-800 number to the place you most need to reach.

Dan tells us that a short sale, in simple terms, means that we'll sell the house for less than we owe, and that if we find a willing buyer who will put in enough capital—say, 75 percent?—the bank will make up the difference. We'll be fine. We'll sell, we'll move on, we'll rent something a block from the beach, something with a tiny yard for the dogs, something without an ugly porch swing on the side yard, something without tenants or stucco or plates on the walls.

We'll all call it square, call it even, call it a bad dream, or a good dream, depending on the way you look at it.

It is early summer. The neighbor's dog is yipping and the bar down the street just opened, and I can hear the faraway jukebox playing Tony Lucca's "Devil Town."

"For now, stop making payments," Dan says. "If you're already in the red, we can push the paperwork faster."

We do it. We stop writing monthly checks and we spend our next free weekend polishing floors, washing windows, fluffing throw pillows. We list the home with a realtor friend, and for every open house, we bake warm cookies and squeeze fresh lemonade, displayed in an artisan pitcher on gleaming granite countertops.

We have a protocol. The request will arrive—*Can we see the house in an hour?*—and the answer is always yes, yes, a hundred yesses. *Ping.* While the cookies bake, Ken scurries around to find errant dust bunnies and smooth the sheets. I light a few candles in the bathroom, check the renter's rooms to be sure towels are off the floor and beds are made. We gather the dogs for a long walk, throw the key under the doormat, and say a quick prayer. "They're chocolate chip," we tell ourselves. "Who wouldn't buy a home with warm chocolate chip cookies?"

The offers pour in, and we accept the highest bid quickly. But there is hesitation in the realtor's voice. "The banks are swamped with paperwork," he says. "I'm going to do everything I can to push this through."

We call Dan with the good news.

Maybe Dan, with the direct number.

Maybe Dan, whom we later discover is no longer employed by our lender as of two and a half days ago.

We are assigned to another agent, another agent who says how sorry she is, but she has other clients whom she has been serving for far longer, and we need to be moved to the bottom of the stack again.

"We're very busy," she says. "It's a really bad time for us all. Expect to hear from me in at least, I don't know, ninety days? Maybe longer?"

We do not have ninety days. We have a buyer paying more than Maybe Dan has agreed to accept, but only if their loan is approved, and only if we move quickly. We have to move quickly.

Why is no one moving quickly?

The slow living philosophy we have worked so hard to adopt is not, in this moment, serving our interests well.

It is July 4th. We have just dined on hotdogs and watermelon, and the sky is turning indigo. The neighborhood parade is over. Our cheeks are rosy, our knees stained from the grass. We are watching our friends' children play in the yard, spelling their names with sparklers swinging through the air in anticipation of the big fireworks show over the pier.

The children are light, carefree, joyful, and I manage to lose myself in their happy spirits, in their childhood innocence—until I don't.

As the sun sets and our fingertips grow cold, I watch Ken pass out a handful of blankets to friends and neighbors. My mind wanders toward our future. *What now? What do we do now?*

"Happy Independence Day," Ken says with a kiss on the cheek. He sits down on the grass next to me as the first fireworks light up a purple sky.

"Are we going to be okay?" I ask him.

"We're going to be better than okay," he says as he reaches for my hand. "We are going to be free."

"We're coming home!" I say to my mother over the phone. It is Sunday night, our weekly check-in. We generally spend our call in a

JULY 4TH '08

state of small-town gossip—*I saw Betty's obituary was in the paper, and didn't you graduate with Sarah Law? She's my new dentist!*—but today, I have news.

It is not every mother's dream to hear that her youngest daughter is sullying her name with a foreclosure at twenty-six years of age, and so I do not share this part. I do not share that the banks are not moving, that we are stuck in a sea of red tape, that we have stopped paying the mortgage on a property the bank won't allow us to sell. I do not share that it seems we are joining the masses of people wading away from perfectly lovely houses, with scattered sheets of adjustable-rate mortgage paperwork floating behind them. I do not share that we have

been advised by a distinguished financial planner and family member to go bankrupt, to start over, that this is going to get much, much worse before it all gets better.

I share, instead, that we are still trying for a short sale, and we are hopeful, but in the meantime, we can push the sale through from the Midwest just as easily, right?

"We'll be home in time for Grandpa's eightieth birthday," I say.

"Erin, are you sure?" she asks. A mother knows what a mother knows.

"Sure, we're sure!" I say with a forced smile. Does she feel it on the other end of the line? Can she hear it in my voice?

But I don't ask those questions. I ask an easier one. "What can I bring to Grandpa's party?"

Our final days as Los Angeles residents are spent bubble-wrapping glassware and reserving Super 8 motel stops from Redondo Beach, California, to Fort Wayne, Indiana.

One night, our tallest friend, Manoj, comes over to help Ken pack but spends the bulk of his time engrossed in a marathon of *America's Next Top Model*. We scream at the videos streaming on my computer— "Fatima! Fatima!"—until Ken sighs heavily, signaling that these boxes aren't going to move themselves.

I saw a rerun of Fatima's season a few months ago, and I thought of Manoj, of that night in a near-empty home, and of the next night when he and his wife, Alexis, packed the remaining boxes, the floor lamps, the laundry baskets of cleaning supplies into our U-Haul while we enjoyed one last dinner with friends.

Friends like this don't change with a zip code, and as our time in LA ends, we find ourselves finally realizing just how rich the season has been. We have been feasting on brioche every breakfast, and here we thought it had all just been toast.

Six months later, Ken and I walk up the

concrete steps to an Indiana courthouse of marble and limestone. We are filing for bankruptcy, and we are not yet thirty years old.

I no longer consider the bankruptcy, the foreclosure, our LA home to be a fault in judgment. We purchased a house in the very wrong place at the very wrong time, and our credit was a casualty.

But by the world's standards, we had failed. Bankruptcy, by definition, means "the state of being completely lacking in a particular quality or value."

Completely lacking, I felt. We had no particular quality or value, other than a single car I'd purchased in college and the contents of the U-Haul we had moved into the driveway of Ken's parents' home.

When you feel this sort of completely lacking, you see the world in a state of less— and not the appealing kind. You see what you do not have, and you don't see what you do.

What we did not have was money, security, a home, a stable job.

What we did have was a second chance. Why hadn't we seen it?

We had a place to sleep. We had a loving family. We had our health.

One of these would be gone in a year.

WHAT I WORE TO THE COURTHOUSE, THE FIRST TIME

My most proficient-looking outfit:

001. White collared button-down shirt
002. Dark skinny jeans
003. Pink blazer
004. Gray, low-heel pumps

00

11.

FORKS UP

And she said gently—that they believe when a lot of things start going wrong all at once, it is to protect something big and lovely that is trying to get itself born—and that this something needs for you to be distracted so that it can be born as perfectly as possible.
—*Anne Lamott,* Traveling Mercies

There were signs.

Once, when my in-laws moved my belongings across the country from Muncie, Indiana, to Hollywood, Ken's dad, Bill, pulled over somewhere in Arizona.

Bill's legs had swelled in such a way that his feet appeared to be tanned marshmallows, the kind you pull from the bonfire just before they burn to black.

"I've gotta take off my shoes," he said. "I think it's the heat."

Another time, when we had already moved home, when we had already begun to wonder if something was irreparably wrong with his father, Ken found Bill in his boxers in the kitchen, pouring salt from the salt-shaker directly into his mouth.

As if it were milk from a carton.

As if it were Junior Mints at the movies.

"I'm hungry," he said. "I'm so hungry."

We accompanied Ken's parents to the hospital and waited in the lobby for test results. Betsy, Ken's mother, was a nurse educator in the hospital, and daily we passed a nurse, a doctor, an anesthesiologist in the hallway and they stopped us. "You guys home for a visit? How's LA?"

Each time, we replied with some small version of the truth we were slowly coming to accept.

We're home for a bit, yeah. We missed the seasons. We missed the family. There weren't any crisp orange leaves in California. How are you?

Once, I ran into a phlebotomist in the cafeteria, telling her that we moved simply because I'd had a sudden and urgent craving for the coney dog stand downtown—extra onions!—and then I smiled and went off to fill my coffee cup.

The doctors were stumped by this rogue illness, this odd disease that caused Ken's father's limbs to fill up with enormous amounts of fluid, that rendered him on some days unable to move, that made him crave such unlikely foods, that made a former ironworker so weak, so sluggish, so small.

He seemed to be fading. He seemed to be fading so fast.

We were to keep an eye on it.

When we finally received an answer, when our gaze was broken with a diagnosis, it was too late. He was ill. It was the bad kind of ill.

Amyloidosis is defined as a rare disease that occurs when abnormal proteins build up in your organs. It is usually produced in the bone marrow and can then be deposited into any tissue or organ.

Deposited.

Deposit.

A transaction, a delivery.

Anything given as security or in part payment.

To be stored for safekeeping.

For Ken's father, the abnormal proteins were deposited into his heart, where they were not stored for safekeeping, where they were not given as security or in part payment, but where we were to "keep an eye on it."

Bill's heart, Ken's brain. Two places meant for safekeeping that were no longer safe.

Our bodies, our homes, our futures, our plans. When they become unsafe for us, where do we rest?

If there is a more humbling act than a twenty-seven-year-old wife sleeping on her grown husband's childhood sheets next to the oak nightstand that holds his high school

OUR BODIES, OUR HOMES, OUR FUTURES, OUR PLANS. WHEN THEY BECOME UNSAFE FOR US, WHERE DO WE REST?

yearbook, next to love letters from old girl-friends, next to a collection of decade-old baseball cards, I have not yet lived it.

Our families all welcome us with open arms. The moment we cross the border into Indiana, weary from our crosscountry road trip, our rental truck heavy with disappointment and old CDs, my dad calls me on my cell phone. "Pull over!" he says. "At the gas station! Look!"

And there my parents are standing, by the air pump at a run-down gas station with a Taco Bell and a KFC, just beaming, just looking as if we hold the sun in the back of our U-Haul.

"Welcome back!" they say kindly, wide hugs and wet eyes.

I've always wondered if that phrase was deliberate. If they'd thought of it ahead of time, if they'd discussed their choice of words over oatmeal that morning. *Welcome to Indiana? No, no, too informal. Welcome home? It's too soon to call it that, Mary.*

Welcome back? Welcome back, yes. That sounds about right. Yes.

Ken's parents are just as joyful to have us home/back, and by the time we reach their driveway winding through the trees, it looks as if they've been standing there for nearly an hour, the sun setting, the mosquitoes humming.

"Just in case you were early," his dad says.

Still, it is not a simple thing to transition from daughter-in-law to roommate. Ken's father is driven half-mad when Bernie pees on the carpet or when I load the dishwasher incorrectly. "Forks up," Ken reminds me, and my solution is not entirely mature, because it is to no longer load the dishwasher at all. Ken and I grew up in families with different standards of cleanliness, and when I forget to squeegee the shower in the morning (and when Ken reminds me that I've forgotten to squeegee the shower in the morning), I grow defensive.

"This isn't easy for me," I say.

"This isn't easy for me either," he says.

It is not all bad, the time living with my in-laws. I brush up on my crossword puzzle game while waiting in the hospital between Bill's appointments, and I can now authoritatively tell you that in crossword puzzles and in life, use pencil.

Things will need to be erased.

Betsy, Ken's tiny blonde mother with polished nails, takes up cooking and we all gain ten pounds eating stuffed peppers with goat cheese, prime rib, and beef stroganoff. When my father-in-law is placed on a strict low-salt diet and is instructed to forgo her culinary experiments, we gather instead around a fresh, delicious salad concoction and he wrinkles his nose.

This isn't easy for me, she might say.

This isn't easy for me either, he might say.

I sometimes place this time period, this brief year and a half, in a category of immense personal growth. It's a humiliating quantification because I realize that when it was over, when everything had changed, when we had all become different, I was still a deeply selfish person.

Once, Ken's mother surprises me with an office in a spare room of her home. Betsy had moved chairs and side tables into the living area to accommodate a long desk with a Tiffany-style table lamp, a plush office chair, and a cheerful houseplant. It is makeshift— "No bells and whistles," she says—but it will do.

It later becomes my favorite place to cry— the plush office chair, the cherrywood desk, the low-pile carpet that has started to fray near the glass french doors. If you angle your head just so, you can see out the front door, past the yard, over the pond, over the rows of pine trees, and into a neighborhood—a life—beyond.

I thank her, grateful to have a space of my own in a house I think holds very little room for me. It never occurs to me that it holds very little room for her either, now that the person who occupies the space beside her in bed is slowly fading away.

12.

ALL THAT REMAINS IS WHAT YOU LOVE

Because I'd like to think I can still summon the total carpe diem, reckless abandon, bulletproof sense of invincibility that I once had wearing that shirt.
—Emily Spivack

In my makeshift office, the one with the cheerful houseplant, a writing assignment comes in from a magazine editor in NYC. "Could you cover a fashion experiment for me?" it reads. "It's called thirty by thirty, or thirty for thirty, or something of the sort? You wear just thirty items for thirty days, a month. What do you think? Google it."

I have just returned from a quick shopping trip. A cheap plastic bag with my purchase in it is on the floor next to my office chair. I was feeling down earlier, Ken's father is not doing well, and I had talked myself into the "reward" of an afternoon trip to Target—a style bandaid for my emotions. With leather sandals, a rope belt, and a floral maxi dress, I nurse my wounds. Eighty dollars in cash, it seems, is a small price to pay for happiness, again.

The feeling is fleeting, of course. It always is. By the time the price tag is clipped and the items are laundered, the shiny and the new wear off and each item becomes just another product of a bad day. Before I can hang the dress in my closet, it already feels worn and dated. Yesterday's discards. It is

difficult to place a value on something that has no value to begin with, no necessary purpose with which to justify its presence.

And so I pause. Can I handle the project? It sounds like a shopping diet, and judging by my binge, I could stand to exercise a bit of self-control.

But it would mean photographing my outfits—*myself*—daily. It would mean stepping in front of the camera, just left of the critics, into the spotlight. And in truth, I have been playing it safe since the bankruptcy, since our Midwest move. I've been hiding behind curated images of geode street art and geometric rugs. I've convinced myself there is nothing beautiful here, nothing lovely to be found in this cherrywood desk in my in-laws' home. Leave the beauty to the experts. To the ones carving miniature sculptures out of a Crayola twenty-four pack. To the ones designing jewelry using junk they find on the beach. I'd rather write their stories. I'd rather share their beauty.

It has been said that one man's trash is another man's treasure, but what has been said of your own trash? Of your own failures? I don't know.

And yet this is the internet. This is a land in which we are all experts, in which there is no economy of beauty, in which there is no shortage of inspiration. This is a land in which a grieving, panicked, bankrupt stylist is offered a voice. This is a land in which we all are offered a voice.

"I'm in," I say to my editor.

And this, you should know, is how I became an unofficial ambassador of the newest trend in fashion/minimalism: the capsule collection.

A capsule collection is created by limiting the contents of your closet. One of its purposes is to disprove the myth that more clothing offers more options. In reality, most of us reach for the same items again and again, and the unused items waste away in our wardrobes.

You reach for the favorite gray linen tee you found in Arizona on that rainy road trip to the badlands, the one on which your sister's dog vomited in the back seat. You reach for the perfect-for-you jeans that are barely surviving—how long have they been in rotation? ten years? fifteen?—held together with only memories of past use. Here, the burn mark on the left cuff from that bonfire night in Malibu. Was that the night of your best friend's proposal? Isn't that right? And there, the red wine stain on the thigh from the

time you brought merlot and glasses to the hospital—it's a boy!—and even the nurses had clinked stemware to the tune of the beeping monitors.

It's simple to start: you spend an afternoon culling your wardrobe until all that remains is what you love.

All that remains is what you love.

Do you love it because it remains?

11.6 years.

Or does it remain because it is loved?

16.7.

The goal is to keep as few items as possible, to encourage you to create multiple options with minimal pieces. To rid yourself of decision fatigue, to edit away the belongings that no longer suit you.

It is a lofty goal, but a worthy one. In closets, you get to choose what to keep.

In life, you don't.

After receiving the details of my assignment, I pad down the scratchy carpeted hallway to Ken's old bedroom for a quick inventory. Cautiously, I thumb through the contents of our shared closet—metal hangers scratching metal rod, *swipe-swipe-swipe*—as I sort the items I'll keep and those I'll store until my extremist experiment is over.

I toss tees from bands that broke up long

ago. I make piles of smart little pencil skirts, proper cardigans, the gauzy Bohemian tunics that covered my shoulders in LA when the city sun sank. I find a lone swimsuit top and think of its missing counterpart, a sad bikini bottom lost in ether.

The afternoon moves quickly with aid from a Mason Jennings CD I find tucked between a pair of Hunter boots, and as the songs play on, I end up with thirty-four of the allotted thirty items.

It's not hard to let the others go. It's not hard to drag three kitchen trash bags full of unloved clothing to the thrift store.

But it is, a little, when you return home to see an emptier closet. It is, a little, when you feel the expanse, the empty, and you wonder if what has been lost needs replacing.

I have not yet tackled my shoe cabinet.

I call an old friend in LA for support and also to whine. "I'm already bored with most of what I chose and I haven't even started. What if I'm seen in the same outfit over and over? Is it odd to show up somewhere, any-where, in the same dress two days in a row? Will everyone think I'm boring?"

Will I?

"I think that what you'll discover more and more as you get older is that most people aren't thinking about you at all." Novelist Haven Kimmel wrote this.

My girlfriend laughs as only girlfriends can do. "Better make sure it's a cute dress," she says, and as we switch topics, I mentally vow to tackle the shoe situation tomorrow. First thing in the morning, I think.

It is day 1 of the great fashion experiment. Thirty items in thirty days, including shoes. I dress in my simplest of outfits—skinny jeans and a striped top—and I tie an olive green headwrap around my hair to buoy my spirits. I look great. It takes roughly three minutes to get dressed.

I can do this, I say to the girl in the mirror.

The next few days prove to be easy, and I applaud myself for my self-control. At my new Bible study, I tell my friend Nancy—a gloriously ornery eighty-eight-year-old—about my extraordinary experiment. She says to me, a blueberry muffin in her mouth, "Wait a minute, you own more than thirty items? Honey, I've never owned more than three pairs of shoes. I can fit the entire con-tents of my closet into a small cooler. I've done it before," she says, "on a pontoon boat."

Elderly women know everything there is to know about everything there is to know.

And then, day 5.

It is raining, and I have a slew of errands to run. There are groceries to purchase, a package to mail. I have not included my favorite waterproof boots in the collection, so I swap out a pair of shoes I haven't yet worn for my rain boots. I think I still haven't broken the rules; I have simply located a nice, warm, waterproof loophole. Technically, it's still thirty items. But then there's that floral dress, the one with the dipping hemline, and it looks so great when paired with the rain boots, and really, I don't want to give up another item in exchange. Thirty-one never hurt anyone, right?

The next week, thirty-one items become thirty-eight, and on day 19, I quit.

I arrive at a handful of justifications for quitting—the hospital's air-conditioning is frigid, to name one of them—but the truth is that I am not ready to learn the far-reaching effects of my consumerist ways.

"Nothing ever goes away until it has taught us what we need to know." Buddhist nun Pema Chodron said this.

All that remains is what you love.

It will be years before I successfully whittle my wardrobe to thirty items or less, for good. But today, the lion is hungry, and it is high noon. Feeding time.

NANCY'S SUMMER CAPSULE WARDROBE

001. Hosiery
002. White sneakers
003. 1 church dress (floral)
004. 1 church skirt (plaid)
005. 1 silk blouse
006. 1 pair of slacks*
007. 1 sun hat
008. 1 swimsuit
009. 1 pair of long shorts
010. 1 T-shirt for gardening
011. 1 T-shirt for errands

I wrote "pants," and Nancy informed me that no, pants were created by the antifeminist movement. "Slacks, honey," she said. "Call them slacks."

13.

MEASURE TWICE, CUT ONCE

It's only after we've lost everything that we're free to do anything.
—*Chuck Palahniuk*

It is unnatural for two recently bankrupt midwesterners to wind up on the front page of HGTV.com with their own online show, and so I will explain.

It is the direct result of my father-in-law's encouragement. One night, I am sprawled on the hospital cot pretending to do crossword puzzles but am instead listening to the monitor beeps, trying to find the rhythm in it all, trying to keep an eye on it, trying to remember what I'm supposed to be looking for.

I make small talk as Bill changes the channel to HGTV to take a break from basketball or MSNBC.

"I'm thinking of pitching a renovation series to their site," I say.

"Make it a show," he says with a rasp. "Go big."

Ken and I have not been going big lately, not since the foreclosure, the short sale, the bankruptcy. We've been going small. We tread lightly with each other, with the world. Most days it is a feat to change out of sweatpants, and when we muster the strength to do that, it is simply to watch *House* reruns in the family room with a bowl of microwave noodles.

When we do go out, to a Friday night

steak dinner with Ken's parents, we walk past our cardboard boxes propped up against garage walls, our treasured belongings that speak of a former life spent in the sun and sand. I gaze at them sometimes, wondering when they'll move to a permanent place. When will we be settled? When will this be over?

What am I looking for?

I miss the art and photography that lined the walls of our home in LA. I miss the abstract art of my friend Jaime. I miss that weird profile of a girl's face where her nose is a chair. I don't know what it means, but it is the kind of art you know means something.

"Maybe we should unpack those boxes," Betsy says once. "It might be fun! There's plenty of room to display your favorites."

But we never do. It would seem too final, too settled.

And we don't feel settled.

Ken's Hollywood accolades seem out of place in suburbia. It is as if he were showing up to a barnraising in an expensive top hat, manhattan in hand, while others tip back cowboy hats and beer. Week after week, he sends resumes to local marketing agencies producing car commercials, mattress sales,

lawyer ads, and week after week, he receives the same responses.

You're overqualified. We're not in the market for someone with your experience. Nice top hat, though. Thanks for coming in.

If Los Angeles is a jungle, this is the forest—dense, dark, and secluded. Few people are interested in a trailblazer from the West, and instead, it seems their focus is on preservation. I believe the locals rather like the trees just the way they are.

(They're lovely trees, after all.)

I am only now considering what it must be like for a man to fall so hard, so fast, that his pride cannot help but follow. The hit takes a toll on both of us, and although we both land on our feet, Ken bears the brunt of the bruising.

Try again this time.

In a luckless world, it is time to make our own luck.

We go big, following the advice of Ken's father. Between doctors' appointments and crossword puzzles, between cycles of laundering those worn childhood sheets, we set aside the pennies we're earning from my blog to save for a house.

Another house?

Another house.

Listen. One can live with their in-laws for only so long before the grace period ends, and it has been, oh, six months? Seven. It is time.

One afternoon, I take a Sharpie to a two-by-four and sketch one of those financial goal thermometer charts. We'll need $75,000, maybe $80,000 to purchase a fixer-upper in the area we love. On this particular afternoon, the red shading on the chart reads $991.45. Minus the burgers for lunch.

We have quite a long way to go.

All that remains is what you love.

You might be wondering how it is possible to earn money from a blog, and so I will give you a simple answer that is not at all simple.

You make it up as you go.

You charge advertising space on your website's sidebar—prime real estate in internet land—to your loyal readers who have a shop on Etsy—perhaps a leather backpack maker in Tel Aviv, a clothing designer from Brooklyn. They will be thrilled with the sales they generate; you will be grateful for the income you receive.

You offer to write guest posts for other blogs, magazines, online publications. You promote your freelance services—lookbook styling, product photography—on your blog and receive steady gigs from independent makers on a budget. You turn your in-laws' basement into a photography studio, a film set, a prop closet.

You write a bio for a ceramicist in Williamsburg. You write an About page for a blogger in New Orleans. You write an online marketing plan for a group of screenprinters in Kansas City.

You launch a course for makers and designers interested in ramping up their online presence. You sell sponsorships for a video web series you produce and promote in which a group of mixed media artists share the struggles, the successes, the sacrifices of the work they do.

You print holiday stationery and sell it, paper-cutting each finger while stuffing a stack of fifteen matte postcards into a cardboard shipping envelope.

You publish dozens of articles with link-baiting titles like "My Eight-Minute Beauty Routine" and "Ten Steps to a Happier You."

You sell a subscription to the independent magazine you launched in LA, and you pitch ad slots between photographs of Parisian polaroids and articles introducing a resurgence of modern wallpaper.

You design patterns for the resurgence of modern wallpaper.

You host a weekend creativity retreat in Portland, you coordinate an annual blogging panel in New York City, you headline a two-day marketing course in San Francisco.

You get carpal tunnel from typing. You get a strained eye from screen time. You get poor posture from sitting on your sofa, on a hospital cot, in a coffee shop, hunched over the keyboard for *just one more email, Ken.*

You work for pennies.

You save the pennies.

You get your house.

MY REAL EIGHT-MINUTE BEAUTY ROUTINE, ON MOST DAYS

Brush my teeth in the shower. Run out of conditioner. Drip soap suds across the bathroom floor to find conditioner in the cabinet; rummage through the cabinet for forty seconds, fail to find conditioner, and accidentally ruin a half-open bag of now-soggy cotton balls in the process. Hop back into the shower, make a mental note to warn Ken about the wet floor, and also remind myself to stop at the drugstore tonight for cotton balls and . . . what was I looking for again?

Ah, conditioner. Today will be a hat day.

Rinse off, towel off, wipe the steam from the mirror. Survey the bags under my eyes and wish I hadn't wiped the steam off the mirror just yet. Concealer, then.

Add styling cream to my tousled bob so my hair looks like it did when I woke up. Lament how much time it takes to make it look as if I've taken no time at all. (So far, seven and a half minutes.)

Slather tinted moisturizer on my face. Think about applying the cat-eye that's all the rage on beauty blogs and in eight-minute morning routines. Stare at liquid liner for twenty seconds before deciding no, no, today is a smudged smoky eye with a swish of mascara day. Rosebud salve for lips. Pinch my cheeks, smile. Nope. Not enough. Add bronzer.

Find hat. Moisturize hands. Get dressed. Grab keys.

Nineteen minutes later, I reserve my final look for the mirror in the hallway, the antique one, the one that's smudged just enough for me to like what I see.

YOUR BEAUTY ROUTINE?

_____

_____

_____

Two months after I sharpied the tip-top of our savings thermometer in bright red, two months after we celebrated over cherry cokes and gas station food, we *clack-clack-clacked* on the marble floors of the same tiled courthouse where we had filed for bankruptcy just over a year prior.

There is a home up for auction, a home we very much think could be our own.

In the lobby of the courthouse, a sheriff greets us. There are seven men and me. I am wearing my second most proficient-looking outfit.

The sheriff's sale begins immediately, and we wait for our property to be introduced in the line-up. Slowly, it becomes clear that many of the men are here for other properties, homes in prosperous areas downtown, buildings with promise.

Surely no one will be interested in our tiny neighborhood fixer-upper?

"Next up: Winterfield Drive," the sheriff announces.

Ken begins with a bid, and it is eerily silent for a moment, and we think that perhaps we're the only ones interested? Perhaps we might pull this thing off? Perhaps we might have our home?

And then one man in shiny boots raises a hand and the race is on.

Ken bids against the booted man. The two nickel-and-dime each other in hundreds, then thousands, and this goes on for one minute, two? Time is syrup. I am sweating in my proficient-looking outfit.

The sheriff grows impatient as he witnesses the exchange, and sensing that something drastic must be done, Ken does it.

"Eighty thousand, final offer."

We wait. The booted man shifts. He thinks. He looks at the sheriff, at Ken, at my capable shoes, the capable black pumps I nearly tossed away in my capsule wardrobe project months before.

He smiles.

"Congratulations," he says, shaking Ken's hand. "I was just gonna flip it. You two'll be real happy there."

Between the working and the hospital, the meetings and the hospital, the conferences and the hospital, Ken and I grow nomadic in spirit. The house on Bent Hollow—Ken's parents' home—holds our toothbrushes, our cardboard boxes, and my makeshift office with the cheerful houseplant. It holds a closet with our clothing, it holds my laptop.

The hospital sometimes holds a few of these things as well—another pair of toothbrushes, an old stick of patchouli deodorant, my laptop—for those rare late nights when we rotate overnight stays in an attempt to catch doctors who might have enough time to explain what is happening to Ken's father, to explain what is happening to our family.

The days are too busy for explanations, but the nights are long. They are quiet. There is plenty of time.

We now have a third home, on Winterfield. It will house Ken's tools, Ken's camera tripod, my computer, a stereo on which to blast Billy Joel's "Uptown Girl" when one is feeling overwhelmed.

We are placing roots, leaving trails in the forest, leaving artifacts in the earth. The toothbrushes, the laptop, the camera tripod, the patchouli deodorant, the cheerful houseplant.

Once, after misplacing my computer's power cord, I drive around from Bent Hollow to the hospital to Winterfield. It is nowhere to be discovered in all three homes. I purchase a new one.

Months later, I find it in the black mesh lining of my luggage, coiling like a snake in the brush. My luggage, of course—the fourth home, the home that promised to take me to the zip code Anywhere but Here.

WHAT I WORE TO THE COURTHOUSE, THE SECOND TIME

001. Light blue collared button-down shirt
002. Black pencil skirt
003. String of pearls
004. Black pumps

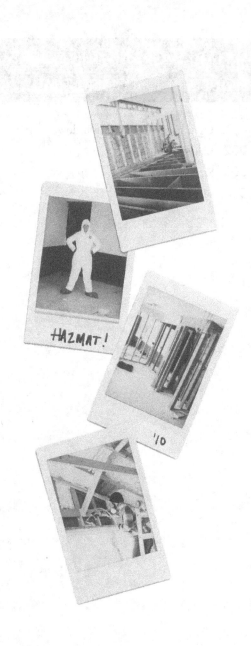

HAZMAT!

'/0

While moving from home to home, while saving our pennies, I had begun putting together a proposal for HGTV.com.

The plan is simple: I will garner press outlets and secure product partners, and I will write weekly updates. HGTV.com will host it and I will promote it on my site. Ken will renovate, and we'll film it all together.

(Simple plans are anything but.)

The idea sells to the network, and I sign the contract for our newest project: a two-year, twenty-four-episode renovation show for HGTV.com.

Our home on Winterfield—a sleepy midwestern ranch nestled in a kid-friendly neighborhood—is a disaster. It is difficult to describe the magnitude of the wreckage, the filth, so I will say this: shortly after our walk through, we find a moldy ham sandwich underneath the oversized flannel sofa.

In the kitchen, just off the dirty-carpeted den, there are old cigarette butts on the counter and empty checkbooks tossed next to bug-infested cereal boxes. One floor below, in the basement, every wall is covered with mold the shade of moss. "We're going to need some hazmat suits," Ken says. He is not kidding.

It is a beautiful wreck.

It is our beautiful wreck.

Have you ever renovated for a length of time? Endured the chaos, the rubble, the stress? In a 2001 *LA Times* article, therapists rank renovation stress in a marriage "somewhere between infidelity and meddling mothers-in-law."

On my own scale of stress management, I will call this a 6.5 level mission. It was not impossible, and it is not a time I am unable to look back on fondly. It was simply a difficult time, and sometimes we confuse difficult times with bad times.

We don the hazmat suits and start fighting, taking breaks along the way to eat hamburgers and change the radio station. I run around tidying corners, corralling tools into piles, finding ways to make myself useful until later it is announced that moving the pliers into an unnamed pile is decidedly *unuseful*.

How does the saying go? The way you tidy a home is the way you deal with a problem?

Ken is a get-your-hands-dirty guy. He once moved a piano down a flight of stairs at 2:00 a.m. using only a pulley, some rope, and his brain. If he doesn't know how to do something, he youtubes it. If he doesn't

know how to fix something, he rolls up his sleeves and tries. He learns, he practices, he perfects. He knows the most important tenet of renovation: that things get messy before they get clean.

And here I am tidying the toolbox.

Here I am hiding the mess.

But there is this one breezy August afternoon in Indiana. Ken's father is in the hospital for testing, and we have rented a basket crane to re-side the front of the house. We estimate the project will take a few days (ever the optimistic duo, we are), and two weeks later, on Ken's birthday, we place the final piece of siding on the tip-top triangle of the roofline. Wearing caulk-stained gloves and with sawdust in our hair, we hum "Happy Birthday" and toast with our Nalgene water bottles from the top of the crane.

Ken has turned thirty.

"He might live to be thirty," the doctor said.

We were meant to keep an eye on it.

He has survived past his expiration date. *We* have survived past his expiration date.

I cannot accurately call this realization one of relief or even surprise. In truth, we hadn't been keeping an eye on it, at least not on the tumor. We'd been keeping an eye on

Ken's father, on rebuilding our lives, on cabinetry measurements and HGTV.com scripts.

Sometimes, when we're not looking for what we want, we find what we need.

On the ground below, leaves somersault. It is almost fall; the season is changing. There is something about the wind, the stillness, the peace. The birds are quieter than usual, like they are whispering tiny goodbyes to one another, exchanging well wishes and change-of-address forms.

Nestled into a swaying basket crane, I recognize the feeling of gratitude. I am grateful for this project, for this challenge, for this season. For the time we stained our floors the wrong shade and the hickory turned a bright yellow tint—school bus style—and Ken spent the next forty-eight hours on his knees, sanding out the mistake. For the time we kept receiving the wrong shower door—was it twice, three times?—and Ken bathed with the backyard hose for weeks. For all of the times Ken and his mother painted, hammered, measured, cut, while Ken's father and I read inky publications (he: car advertisements; me: *Real Simple*) in the hospital.

For all of the times we missed the mark in budget, in execution, in timing.

For all of the times I missed the mark in grace, in love, in perspective.

Ken's blood, our sweat, my tears. On Winterfield, on Bent Hollow, at the hospital, we worked to build something amid the rubble. With every wall that came down on the project house, another round of my father-in-law's test results returned. No progress. Fewer answers. No cure.

Ken's father will die before he sees the end of our renovation project.

Ken will not.

I write my father-in-law a eulogy that I read to no one. It speaks of the basket crane, the trees, the crisp August evening when he was still alive, still in testing. It speaks of what I came to know on that day, of what

SOMETIMES, WHEN WE'RE NOT LOOKING FOR WHAT WE WANT, WE FIND WHAT WE NEED.

loving him taught me about the fleeting feeling of happiness and the enduring work of gratitude. It speaks of his laugh, the one that folded him in two.

One of Bill's favorite phrases is an old work adage he passed around with his ironworking crew. Sometimes he brought the advice home, teasing Betsy mercilessly as she trimmed hair in the kitchen on a Saturday morning, a bleached towel draped around the neck.

"Measure twice; cut once."

It now seems to me a cruel truth that Ken had to measure his own years, then measure his father's years, then . . .

Cut.

Now it is Ken who says this.

Measure twice; cut once.

This is his phrase now. I hear him say it each time he begins a project, each time he pulls on Bill's old work gloves, which still smell faintly of rebar and patchouli.

But only faintly.

Once, on a trip to the redwoods, Bill told us how these trees are older than humans, how they dated back nearly two thousand years. "That's some legacy, yeah?" he said. We walked and chatted and stopped to read the information signs, soaking up facts along the way. Later, we ate a picnic near the gift shop, and after finishing turkey on wheat, Bill sneaked in to buy a few redwood seeds for his back yard.

"No way they could grow in an Indiana climate," he said with a smile. "But you never know!"

He never did get a chance to plant them, or to try. But Ken kept the seeds in his glove compartment, and every now and then, we'll look for a tissue or hand sanitizer, and the plastic bag will fall to the floor. "Redwoods, 2007," it reads in a black Sharpie, written in the cursive we miss most.

Bill's life taught us much.

But his death taught us more. His death taught us that today is a gift, and that gifts are not meant to be portioned. That counting our time on both hands, circling expiration dates on calendars, questioning our own destinies—11.6 years or 16.7?—that none of these methods will add years to our lives or lightness to our souls.

Gratitude cannot add years either, of course. No method of human strength, of sheer will, can change the fate we're offered.

But changing our fates and changing our lives are two very different things.

And if it is a changed life I am after, gratitude seems a good place to start.

After Bill's death—after the hospice and the viewing, after the funeral luncheon with lemon cookies, Ken and I take our time returning to the renovation project. We ease in with a mundane DIY project—a modern mailbox makeover—something simple, something short. Our minds are elsewhere as we lay tarp on the front lawn and disassemble the parts for spray-painting.

And it is on this afternoon that a neighboring couple walking their dogs stop to chat. Because our home is in such poor condition, it isn't out of the ordinary for passersby to stop and note any improvement: new siding, roof work, landscaping. Once, while Ken was spraying weeds on a hot spring morning, the HOA secretary pulled over her Buick and rolled down the window. "Yard's lookin' good, Ken! Careful, there's some buried cats in the side yard, over by those rocks. Yep, right there! Okay, see ya at Tuesday's meeting!"

Most days, we don't mind the interruptions. Even with a deadline, the distractions are sometimes nice.

Today is one of those days.

"Hey, did you guys know you've got a redwood in your back yard?" the man says, his beagle pulling on the leash. "Only one I've ever seen round here. Must be a hundred years old at least."

We didn't know. We couldn't have known.

My eyes fill with tears as the man continues down the sidewalk, and I want nothing more than to call my father-in-law and tell him his very favorite tree is standing there—tall, proud—right in our back yard. *Come over! Come see! Can you believe it? All along? All this time?*

But I think he already knows.

BUT CHANGING OUR FATES AND CHANGING OUR LIVES ARE TWO VERY DIFFERENT THINGS.

I no longer speak of Ken's tumor as an expiration date.

People don't expire, not really. Their traces linger far past our flat calendar squares. Their fingerprints outlive our feeble clock's hands. Their work gloves and work phrases do too.

The seeds they plant become trees—tall, proud—providing shelter for tomorrow, shade for today. Legacies for a hundred years more.

And the seeds they didn't get a chance to plant?

Well, I suppose it's our turn for those.

14.

ENOUGH SPACE TO GROW A REDWOOD

And a step backward, after making a wrong turn,
is a step in the right direction.
—Kurt Vonnegut

Ken's father left more than a legacy, more than a redwood seed. His advice from the hospital bed—"Go big"—turns out to be right; the online show is successful. Readers download episodes of Ken surprising me with a Scandinavian-inspired fireplace. We share blooper reels and paint colors and tutorials to create a rustic headboard in an afternoon.

Once, in my local Bed, Bath and Beyond, the checkout clerks begin whispering as I approach the counter. "Is this for your show?" the bolder one with the pierc-ings asks me as he gestures toward the tower of linens I am holding.

I am caught off guard, because I have come to think of it not as a show but merely as what we do between meals. I blush and I nod, and I deflect with a compliment on his bluebird tattoo, and now it's his turn to blush. As it turns out, if you have a show on HGTV.com, you might receive discounted white sheets from your local retailers. It is quite a nice perk, worth noting.

Our home becomes a studio. Every junk drawer must be tidied, every boot scuff

photoshopped, every sheepskin fluffed. Little by little, we renovate each room to perfection. Ken lays the hickory floorboards; I reposition the ottomans. Ken installs white cabinetry with sleek silver pulls; I style the countertops with soy candles and wooden cutting boards. Ken builds an oak plank dining room table; I throw a dinner party with Heath Ceramics dishes and rose gold flatware.

He does the heavy lifting; I step in for the spitshine.

If our home has become a studio, what does that make us? Are we directors? Actors? Or are we bit players in a film with no end?

Once, shortly after having a baby, Ken's cousin Jess comes to see the progress. We give her a tour of the hallway construction, the new bathroom shower, the cedar sauna just off the master bedroom. All is white. All is scrubbed. All is tidied.

All is perfect.

Until it is not. Until Jess's baby vomits profusely on freshly laid carpet that is, of course, the color of snow.

"I'm so sorry!" she says, flustered. She gathers towels as Ken hunts down the cleaning solution, and for a brief moment, I am surprised by my own reaction.

It is not of frustration.

It is of *relief.*

Our perfect white house, our perfect white studio, our perfectly fluffed nest has been sullied. It has been stained, and it is no longer perfect. We no longer have to anticipate the moment it becomes less than. It is less than, and it is okay.

"It was bound to happen sooner or later," I say to Jess. "It's okay, really!"

And I mean it.

Three months after a series has been launched, it's time for a hefty wave of promotional efforts. A rule in the world of online publishing states something of this sort, that you have approximately three months to prove your entertaining quips and dazzling tutorials have value, and after three months, the wave of momentum will either continue or crash.

And this is why I visit Brooklyn for two weeks of NYC meetings, for two weeks of NYC events, for two weeks of NYC press interviews. To avoid the crash. Ken stays home to renovate—there is always a deadline, after all—and I trudge forward, eating pizza and getting blisters and shooing away the cats in my friend's apartment complex.

Have you ever been to New York during a hot summer? Have you ever slept in your underwear on an itchy tweed sofa in front of an open window where bustling opportunists visit garbage bins—*slam, beep, boom*—every morning? Has a city like that ever awakened you?

It awakened me like a splash of cold water.

I hadn't even realized I was asleep—or thirsty.

There is something to be said for the way I am using the word *awakened.* We think of an awakening as a positive experience, as if we're enlightened, as if we've become wrinkled and wise in an instant—tiny little transcendent Buddhas. *We have been awakened! We are one with the stars!*

But my awakening, the enlightenment I speak of, was not like this.

You can understand how, in my season of subtraction, of stripping, of hitting rock bottom—the foreclosure, the bankruptcy, the death of a parent—I craved addition. You can feel how I sought wholeness, achievement, contentment.

You can see how I was an age-old Eve, an age-old Adam. You can see how badly I wanted a bite of Eden's apple, to taste knowledge and to swallow it as if it were truth.

You can see how I believed that one bite, one alone, might satiate the hunger. Might fill the void. Might tame the lion.

But the thing about apples is that we're always biting off more than we can chew.

It is hard to see which bites might nourish and which might cause us to choke.

On the day of my awakening, at a press junket celebrating HGTV's newest online channel, a short woman with my mother's haircut hands me a glass of red wine. "You, my dear," she says, "are going to be a household name. Mark my words."

I smile, flattered, and introduce myself.

"I know who you are," she says. "I'm with HGTV."

And now I am simply embarrassed.

I am introduced, then, to a slew of faceless network agents and producers and I shake hands down the line as we chatter about weather patterns and the NYC heat. The executives are each lovely and kind, very well versed in small talk. All are dressed in black, like stark little marks punctuating the two worlds in which I live.

In the Midwest, if you're dressed in black, you're on your way to a funeral.

In New York City, if you're dressed in black, you're on your way to brunch.

The conversation inevitably, after a short time, in a quick changing of the wind, turns to my future. These executives are not new to this expertly choreographed waltz, and I shift on my shiny patent heels as I see the path I am on, bread crumbs of money, power, respect leading to a dense forest of fame and accolades.

But at this press junket, on this NYC rooftop, in these shiny patent heels, it feels like this: They aren't talking *to* me. They are talking *through* me, as if I were invisible or less than whole, like maybe I haven't yet been fully formed in their presence.

Yet.

Or maybe it is just me. Maybe I am the one who doesn't quite know where to look.

BUT THE THING ABOUT APPLES IS THAT WE'RE ALWAYS BITING OFF MORE THAN WE CAN CHEW. IT IS HARD TO SEE WHICH BITES MIGHT NOURISH AND WHICH MIGHT CAUSE US TO CHOKE.

We say goodbye—I have a flight to catch—and a producer pulls me aside. "When you're ready for your show, here's my card," he says. "My cell is on the back. We've got a round of pitches next month and we need to move quickly on this."

As Adam hammers nails on our renovation house miles away, Eve is offered an apple.

On the cab ride to the airport, as I turn the business card over and over in my peach manicured fingers, my cab passes a cemetery where white tombstones are arranged like tight rows of dominoes, stacked up, lined up, ready to tumble over with the touch of a giant's finger. The cab jostles us along and the cemetery whooshes by and I know, simply, in that instant that I do not want this for myself.

I do not want to be stacked, even in death, up against another with so very little room to breathe. I do not want to compete. I want white space. I want room for grace.

Give me, then, the basket crane. Give me the cheerful houseplant, the beef stroganoff, the 10 percent discount on inexpensive white sheets.

Give me enough space to grow a redwood.

I do not take the apple.

Back in Indiana, back on Winterfield, I pull my car into the driveway and see Ken stripping the beams of the back porch. The sun is low; his work gloves are stained. He looks tired.

I read once that the stripping, the sanding, the subtracting—this is the key to a good paint job. This is the key to a seamless varnish.

This is the key to a strong finish.

That sounds right, doesn't it?

Try again this time.

I drop my luggage off at the door and walk around the side of the house for a hug. The heels I'd worn through the airport dig into the lawn, making polka dots across the grass.

Ken asks about my week and I ask about his, and we take a break to let the sun set. It needs no help from us, of course, but certain things just call for an audience. Sometimes one can't help but marvel at the descent.

"What color are you thinking for the paint?" he asks as we head inside to forage through the fridge.

"Something simple," I say. "Something light."

Here is the secret to subtraction.

It doesn't matter what you remove. What matters is that you stop adding it back.

15.

A SYNONYM FOR PERFECT

What's great about this country is America started the tradition where the richest consumers buy essentially the same things as the poorest. You can be watching TV and see Coca-Cola, and you can know that the President drinks Coke, Liz Taylor drinks Coke, and just think, you can drink Coke, too. A Coke is a Coke and no amount of money can get you a better Coke than the one the bum on the corner is drinking. All the Cokes are the same and all the Cokes are good.
—Andy Warhol

I am happy with my decision. Ken is happy with my decision. We have agreed on a number of occasions that the life of fame is not one we would choose, if given the opportunity, and here we are, given the opportunity.

"Am I crazy not to pursue this?" I ask him.

"Just crazy enough," he says.

I have grown comfortable with a slower life, with flying just below the radar, like a bird that has been set free. But flying just below the radar is tricky too, because every now and then you forget the reasons you have taken this route. Every now and then, you look up near the blinding sun to see a flock of geese who are flying higher, stronger, faster, and would you look at that confidence? That formation? That grace?

It looks beautiful, doesn't it?

It looks better.

Doesn't it?

In an air-conditioned hotel lobby bar at a conference for media content creators, I find myself seated at a large mahogany table with a few colleagues, speakers, friends, acquaintances. It's late, so we begin charging creature comforts to our rooms—french fries and wine for some, pie and decaf for others—as the conversation weaves in and out of industry subjects—*Do you keep a strict editorial calendar? What program do you use for tracking analytics? How are you quantifying audience engagement?* After a brief lull in trade talk, a man named Ben who was born and raised in Des Moines, Iowa, leans forward and props his elbows on the table. He speaks softly to the group.

"I made something. Can you guys beta test it for me?"

It doesn't seem like a question, as I am remembering it. It seems rhetorical. Of course we say yes. This is the internet.

The something is Pinterest, the website created to organize, manage, and curate products and ideas on virtual pinboards. As I am writing this very paragraph, there are roughly seventy million users relying on Pinterest to find and share home improvement projects, outfit ideas, recipes, and inspirational quotes. Ben and his cofounders now have more than five hundred employees, with offices in ten major cities worldwide. Pinterest has, in short, transformed the way we find and store information online.

Along the way, it has transformed everything else.

If you ask a woman about the standards and expectations of today's culture, you will likely hear her reference Pinterest in some manner. She found her child's birthday dessert on Pinterest—an extravagant rainbow-layered and tiered cake—although her own version fell remarkably short in a technicolored tower of Pisa. She siphons, almost daily, pages of inspirational pins, from women in boyfriend jeans and heels walking midstride across a sunlit city block to Swedish apartment lofts featuring glossy white floors and breezy open windows. She, just this morning, is seeking new recipes for this week's meal preparation, *but oh, look, wait—are those sandals on sale?*

Pinterest is a mother-in-law whispering in your ear, *Did you see that Thanksgiving tablescape, the one with the backyard foliage that was spray-painted a metallic gold, the one*

WHO COULD HAVE KNOWN THAT MORE
WOULD MAKE US FEEL LIKE LESS?

*with the placecards made from avocado pits,
the one where they're serving those delicious-
looking sweet potato croquettes?*

Pinterest has, in a few short years, become
an addicting escape, an impossible standard,
an invaluable resource. A synonym for perfect.

You cannot blame Pinterest. Who could
have harnessed the great power of a collec-
tive society in search of everything it ever
needed, anything it ever wanted? Who could
have seen the downside as we pressed our
noses to the screen, eyes widening with wonder, watching as our dreams scrolled by, pin
after pin after pin?

Who could have known that more isn't
what we truly need?

Who could have known that more
would make us feel like less?

So I am an early ambassador for this
platform, this machine, this tool. (You can't
shoot the messenger.)

I find the site to be an incredible business tool for cataloging future projects, for
finding and keeping photography tutorials,

for easily bookmarking visual ideas and discovering new artists to interview. With the
wrapping up of our HGTV.com show, with
the decision not to pursue a TV contract, I
am back to my blogging roots full-time.

I do not, not in the beginning, consider
Pinterest for personal purposes. I can't predict
the mass appeal of collecting party inspiration,
decorating resources, style advice. I think of
it only as an industry tool, something to aid
in workflow and update my antiquated bookmarking system. I am a blogger, after all, and
I am well versed in compartmentalization—
online is for work; offline is for play.

In a few months, Ken's aunt, an insur-
ance adjuster in middle America, will corner
me on a lazy weekend at my mother-in-law's
pool. "My cousin just called from Texas," she
says. "She saw your yellow kitchen pendants
on her Pinterest feed!"

"Wait, your cousin from Texas is on Pinterest?" I ask. This is the first memory I have of
the merging of my two worlds: Erin Loechner
and @erinloechner. This is the first memory I

SOME THINGS I HAVE PINNED

001. The "But First, Coffee" Tee (Twice)
002. Seven Ways to Look More Awake without Makeup
003. A DIY Potato Print Table Runner
004. Infused Water Detox Recipe, or Nine Ways to Make Your Water Not Taste Like Water
005. A DIY Copper Pipe Ladder
006. Nine Secret iPhone Tricks That Everyone Else Knows
007. A $4,900 Evening Gown Closely Resembling My Fifth-Grade Jazz Costume
008. Two-Tone Wax Canvas Backpack
009. Coconut-Based Dish Soap
010. A Single Pair of Children's Socks That Cost More Than Most Adults' Shoes
011. Ten Reasons You *Can* Wear White after Labor Day

AND YOU?

_____
_____
_____
_____
_____

have of what I do—write online—becoming mainstream enough to warrant acknowledgment from Ken's aunt's cousin from Texas, from my neighbor's dog-sitter in Nebraska, from my dentist's sister-in-law in Minnesota.

"Wake up," my aunt says. "Everyone is on Pinterest."

She is right. Everyone is on Pinterest. In a few short months, my audience grows from a handful of faithful blog readers to more than one million strangers craving the latest visual inspiration from across the globe.

I have never been one to ignore a craving, and so I provide. I feed the machine, the frenzy, the lion. I upload images of my home—white walls, graphic artwork, mixed throw pillows placed just so in effortless effort. I offer DIY tutorials—"A Modern Floor Lamp in Five Easy Steps!"—and I watch the numbers, the comments, the likes. I watch them grow.

In the name of inspiration, in the name of "giving the people what they want," I add. I provide. I create. I think nothing of the underbelly, the downside, the potentially damaging effects of a society fueled by Pinterest.

But pins prick. They're not for everyone.

They might be for you, though. You who last week stumbled upon a modern nursery displaying a gallery wall of animals photographed by Sharon Montrose. You who are now inspired to redecorate your daughter's room—to discard the bamboo blinds you have salvaged and purchase new Bohemian curtains. A trip to IKEA for sheepskin rugs is in order, and while you're there, you'll need those Ribba frames. Now, where to put the crib? The wallpaper? The antique chandelier?

Me too.

Deep breath.

Are we all inhaling intoxicating Pinterest fumes? An oxygenated reality?

And if so, can we call it true inspiration? The definition of inspiration is the drawing of breath, an inhalation, a gasp. A filling-up that offers an abundance of energy for your day, for the task, for that project, for this life.

Are we being inspired when we are meant to inspire?

Are we being inhaled when we are meant to inhale?

Pinterest has contributed to a society of hopeful expectation. There is always a better idea, a quicker solution, an available tutorial, and there is always more to be done. There is always a newer product to discover.

There is always a snack upon which your lion can feed.

But sometimes we're meant to close our eyes, to inhale and exhale, to breathe in and breathe out. Sometimes the best we can do is to shut our eyes to the pink Smeg on Pinterest and open our eyes to our dated white fridge, the smudgy one with our dentist appointment reminder, the report cards, our grandmother's pickle recipe.

Because I can tell you one thing that I know to be true. There is no better Pinterest recipe than your grandmother's pickles.

When you work online, when your livelihood comes from the stories you share and the photographs you take and the ideas you generate, you begin to see yourself as one-dimensional, a girl on the screen.

You receive a slew of comments in any given moment, comments that sing your praises. *Your house is lovely! Your countertops are so clean! I love the eucalyptus branch in the shower!*

You will not explain that you have added the eucalyptus branch in the shower for the photos alone, that it does not remain there on the regular, but you begin to think that perhaps if it did, perhaps if it were a daily affair, perhaps then the comments would be true? Perhaps then your house would be lovely? Perhaps then *you* would be lovely?

This is the beginning of the damage. This is the creation of an unrealistic yardstick, and this is the beginning of you against the wall, tiptoeing in your gym socks, shoulders back, head high, to see if you measure up to the height you are believed to be.

The woman on the screen is extraordinary.

The woman in the mirror is not.

How long before the jig is up? How long before I will be revealed as the poser that I am? How long before the hypocrisy shines through?

You believe that if you had a particular set of throw pillows—the indigo dip-dyed ones you saw on Pinterest last week—you could keep up this facade. With the throw pillows, the clean countertops, the eucalyptus branch—with these, you will *deserve* the recognition you have been given. You will deserve this immense audience that has come to your corner of the internet—this unintentional soapbox that has been styled just so—and you will finally be able to sleep at night. You will have arrived, you will have conquered, your real-life presence will finally grow into your online presence, and look, the skin fits perfectly. Can you smell the eucalyptus from over there? Good.

I am using the word *deserve*, but I am not convinced it is the correct one. We all deserve very little, nothing at all, because if gifts were based on merit, if fame or fortune weren't a cold soup of hard work and timing and sheer dumb luck—and, I believe in many circumstances, the hand of God—well, then, where would the single mother working overnight shifts at the laundromat be? Merit she has. Hard work she has. Timing and sheer dumb luck she has not been granted.

And so, the word *deserve* aside, here I am with the eucalyptus. Here I am amassing dip-dyed throw pillows. Here I am believing that the shoe must fit, that perfection must exist as it does on the screen, and that I must close the wide sweeping gap between the online version of myself and the real me.

The girl on the screen? Surely her bathroom sink doesn't showcase a light ring of pink mold around the drain. Surely her lawn is freshly manicured. Surely she doesn't battle cellulite or frizz or self-doubt on the regular.

She does. (I do.)

When I measure, when I stand on my tiptoes, when I replace the eucalyptus branch, I am telling myself that my flaws need fixing. I am telling myself that I must live up to the one-dimensional world I've created for myself, the one where projects are wrapped up in nice, perfectly cropped before and after squares.

If the pink mold were scrubbed away, would I feel more whole?

If the lawn were cut, the cellulite gone, the frizz managed? Would I become the woman the online world sees?

Will I ever?

Will you?

Math is a bit funny in this way. We can subtract, by choice or circumstance, but with every subtraction, a new addition arrives.

So really, it's not math at all. It's more like sorcery. Smoke and mirrors.

I am no longer shoveling cash into a stucco townhome. I am no longer feeling as if I'm wasting hours, days, lives, working toward an American dream I do not want. I am no longer crying in the master bedroom closet, no longer battling panic attacks, no longer second-guessing exits on the 405.

But the measuring stick is still there.

Of course it is. When you scale the very mountain you fell from, when you rise up and dust off your knees, when you climb with calloused feet, when you suddenly reach the top again, the view remains unchanged.

You will see what you already have seen.

Did you think the lion was sleeping because he did not roar?

16.

WHERE THERE IS BRUISING

*But that's how it is when you start wanting to have things. Now, I just look
at them, and when I go away I carry them in my head. Then my hands
are always free, because I don't have to carry a suitcase.*
—*Tove Jansson*, Comet in Moominland

It is Tuesday. I am scheduled to teach a social media course via a live telecast conference in Berlin this weekend, and I have begun to draft my talk. I sift through my inbox to find my allotted time when I spot an email, buried and unread in bold-faced type. Subject line: Ethiopia?

I am intrigued. I open the message and scan the words to see an invitation, the kind you feel first in your feet and then in your gut and only then do you feel it in your heart and at last, finally, altogether in your head. "Tastemaker trip in August . . . FashionABLE scarves . . . Addis Ababa . . . can you come?"

And this is how I arrive in the domain of coffee and Amharic, and this is how I begin to be changed for good.

We have landed, and it looks different. Laundry hangs on wires pulled taut between cracked windows. The ground is not green and lush but a pink-hued clay of dusty pebbles. Goats roam through makeshift streets,

ETHIOPIA —

and every now and then a whole herd of them stops to graze as traffic halts. Time, I can see, is of no matter in this land.

But the sky, the sky is one I know. It is blue, and it is marbled gray. It is the same as my own.

It begins to grow dark. In a few short hours we will creep through the streets with scarves on our heads. We will see despair and hope and deep longing in young women standing on corners—so many women, so many corners—offering affection in exchange for a quarter.

Ethiopia is rocky. It is unstable. It is a place of momentary happiness and unfathomable setbacks. It is a place of less.

And yet. Through the fabric covering my head, I can see more.

I can see love.

"She likes your nail polish," our translator says.

We are here to enjoy a coffee ceremony, to roast beans, to sing. Our backpacks are weighted by bottled water and phones, and we plop down to learn of the simple pleasures in life.

Pleasures is a stretch, perhaps. I will not pretend to know the hardships this country faces; I am but a tourist. I do not understand what it is like to live in a place where a drink of clean water is not readily available, where education is not accessible, where my basic needs are either not met or fought for with every ounce of my being.

Where I live, we are after silver spoons. Here, there is no soup to slurp.

And so *pleasure* is perhaps the wrong word. But *simple* is the right word, and there is something about the way the two sound together that best describes what I am getting at.

"We've brought some," I say to the translator, holding up a bottle of polish I've recovered from my hefty backpack. I smile and point to a woman's weathered hands. "Would you like me to paint your nails before we have coffee?" I ask.

The woman—her name is Genet—smiles wide with crinkled eyes. She grabs the mint-green polish, quickly twists the cap, and begins to paint my fingertips in wide, messy strokes. I allow her, unsure of how to tell her that I'd intended for it to be the other way around. I'd wanted to paint *her* nails, to thank her in some small imperfect way for the past few days, for changing my mind about beauty.

I'd been raised to think of beauty as perfection, an arrival point, an effortless destination. An after.

It is not, of course, perfection. Beauty is fought for, and the bruising is plenty.

But where there is bruising, there is tenderness.

Genet finishes quickly with great gusto, and she rises to begin roasting our coffee beans. "No, no, no!" I say with swinging hand gestures. "Your turn!"

She hesitates, and I hope I have not offended her.

But she smiles, and she holds out her thumb first, and then her pinky, and then the remaining fingers of her left hand before holding out her right, all at once, splayed wide like a bouquet. I tell the translator that I'd like to put on two coats of polish, if she'd like. If Genet has time?

"It'll last longer," I say.

Soon after, our manicures are finished. They are smudged and shaky, just like us. Blurred and beautiful. Later, we will sip coffee into the night. We will sing. We will dance. We will leave with new hands.

All that remains is what you love.

On the flight home to the States, I scribble on the back of my boarding pass, my polish just beginning to chip away.

"Tuesday. Genet. Manicure. Beauty is not found in the after. It's in the during."

It takes only one visit to a third world country to understand how far I've gone off course.

It takes only one glimpse of the happy sparkle in the eyes of a chocolate woman laughing as she dyes fabric with calloused hands to know I do not understand joy.

Try again this time.

It takes only one visit to a roomful of sex trafficking survivors singing, dancing, swaying as they chop avocados for guacamole to know I do not understand gratitude.

It takes only one peek at a child's singular toy, a helicopter made from a trashed cell phone minutes card and a lollipop stick, to know I do not understand creativity.

All that remains is what you love.

Three weeks later, I am writing in a coffee shop in San Diego, where the atmosphere is one of discontent. It is raining. A gaggle of women with the same handbag exchange woes like a game of poker: *I'll take your remodeling and raise you parenting. I'll see your parenting and raise you aging. (Fold.)* Businessmen in ties and shiny shoes two tables over lament a deal that fell through. *Life offers no deals*, I think, recounting the past few deals that have fallen through in my own life, recounting the past hundred deals that have never even been offered to my Ethiopian friends.

Molehills into mountains, this is our offering. We are clothed. We are fed. We are sheltered. We are stressed?

An Arabian anecdote speaks of a man who loads his camel with a staggering amount of goods for the market. He piles, piles, and piles more until finally, one single wisp of straw sends the camel crashing down. The camel has broken its back.

I look around this urban coffee shop and see the camels, the heavy straw, the broken backs all around me. We are weary. We have burdened ourselves with an inordinate amount of possessions, packed social calendars, busy work schedules—loads that are far too heavy for us to carry—and yet we grip them with clenched hands. More straw, we think. Just one more piece.

"Look at the birds of the air; they do not sow or reap or store away in barns, and yet your heavenly Father feeds them. Are you not much more valuable than they?"

Jesus said this in Matthew 6:26.

I have not yet told you why I am in San Diego. I am filming a commercial for an international home furnishings brand that is known worldwide for inexpensive white bookshelves and meatballs. Yes, yes, they are on Pinterest.

While my Ethiopian friends are weaving handmade scarves to sell so they can send their children to school, I am encouraging those watching to upgrade their outdated kitchens with glass doors and under-cabinet lighting. *Come! Shop! Buy! Don't forget an ice-cream cone on your way out!*

I am having a very difficult time with this.

When we break for lunch, the crew is served food from the cafe. Pita sandwiches, poppy-seed salad, baked chips, fresh cookies. I eat a small portion—I haven't had much of an appetite lately. The overage of food is discarded into a shiny garbage bin in the corner.

Collectively, we fill up the whole thing. *The salad won't keep*, I justify.

Later, I return to my lines. I stress the importance of a new mattress for your best night's sleep. While my lips are talking thread counts, my mind is remembering the girls who were stolen in the Ethiopian night. For them, there is no good night's sleep. There is no promise of tomorrow.

I am having a very difficult time with this.

I tout the benefits of art in the home, the benefits of pattern mixing, the benefits of color stories, the benefits of inspiration. There it is, that word again.

Inhale.

"A fresh coat of paint will revamp any space!" I say in my smart blue dress, and I think of the peeling plaster in the huts of Addis Ababa, nearly ten thousand miles away.

As we wrap for the day, I survey the racks of closets, shoes, accessories we have stored in the dressing room for tomorrow. I think of the mattress, of the paint, of the under-cabinet lighting. I think of the excess.

These things matter.

A comfortable mattress matters to me. A fresh coat of paint matters to me. Under-cabinet lighting matters to me.

I do not want them to matter to me.

But they do.

I am having a very difficult time with this too.

On the cab ride home, I rest my pounding head on cool glass. I peer out the window to watch the birds circling above and flitting around, energized by the setting sun. They have surrendered their loads. They are free in the sky, roaming untethered and cageless. They will not sow or reap.

I think, then, of myself. I think of the weight I carry to pad myself from need or discomfort or boredom. I think of the homes we build like birdcages with garage doors, and I

THERE IS ONLY TODAY, WITH HOLES IN OUR POCKETS, WITH TIME SPILLING OUT. WE CANNOT KEEP IT FOR TOMORROW. WE CANNOT MEND OUR SEAMS TO HOARD, SAVE, CARRY.

think of how we roam this earthly, privileged soil directionless in a sea of more. I think of all of us, weary in our suburban coffee shops, amassing everything my friends in Ethiopia need but having nothing they want.

They have joy. Gratitude. Love. Community. Forgiveness.

We have wicker basket organizers, SUVs, and backyard fire pits.

All that remains is what I love.

Ask an Ethiopian what they need and they might tell you with a wide smile: amassing is meaningless. There is only today, with holes in our pockets, with time spilling out. We cannot keep it for tomorrow. We cannot mend our seams to hoard, save, carry.

Ask a bird how to fly, and it might tell you to remove the weight from your wings.

17.

REMOVING THE WEIGHT FROM OUR WINGS

I was part of that strange race of people aptly described as spending their lives doing things they detest, to make money they don't want, to buy things they don't need, to impress people they don't like.
—*Emile Gauvreau*

It was never a question of need. It was a question of power.

As a child, I was frugal. My parents are frugal, and they taught me the value of hand-me-downs, of upcycling, of squeezing every last drop of the lemon. Together we lived free of consumerism, weekends void of acquisition.

This does not mean I never envied my friends who continually modeled the latest fashion, but it does mean I learned to get creative with what I had. A chiffon scarf, I found, could be a belt on Monday, a headscarf on Tuesday, a tunic on Wednesday, a backpack accent on Thursday, and just that—a chiffon scarf to drape around my neck in chemistry class on Friday.

I did not have a stressful childhood. It was, looking back, blissful.

There were trips to garage sales and thrift stores when necessary, and on birthdays and holidays, between forkfuls of strawberry cheesecake, my sisters and I were each given something new (with tags!).

LIFE LESSONS FROM
A FRUGAL MOTHER

001. It's not a sale if you don't need it. (It's on sale *because* no one needs it. Exhibit A, chain wallets. Exhibit B, toe rings. Exhibit C, Zubaz pants.)

002. Never buy anything dry clean only. There's a reason your dry cleaner drives a BMW.

003. A handmade gift costs less and means more.

004. Don't be afraid of that thrift store musk. It'll wash right out.

005. At a restaurant, order water with lemon. Add in a free sugar packet from the table and do you see it? Free lemonade!

006. You can save time, or you can save money. Shopping unnecessarily saves neither. Penny loafers save both. No laces to tie in the morning, plus an extra two cents for a rainy day.

007. Reduce, reuse, or just plain go without. Embrace minimalism. The less you have to dust, the less you have to dust, am I right?

008. Creativity will forever be in fashion. (Unless it's dry clean only.)

009. If it costs more than a house and is not a house, do not buy it.

010. Live within your means.

See? Blissful.

Frugality is a blessing for me. I am predisposed to love style, prone to seek refuge by rearranging furniture and dreaming of paint chip colors for a quick, cheap, and easy room makeover. I learned early that style is free, that it costs nothing at all, that good taste can transform a home quicker than a million-dollar budget.

Years ago, I was a bathhouse attendant at the local pool. This first job offered me my own income, my independence, and I saved the bulk of my paycheck while still allowing myself a purchase I considered to be so frivolous, so deeply unnecessary, so altogether supreme.

Bonne Bell lip balm, Dr Pepper flavored.

The rush of those early shopping trips still astounds me. I do not understand it. I do not understand my desire for acquiring, because it did not come from my parents, my upbringing, my small-town community.

I know only this: I believe the feeling is one of empowerment. I believe there is something mighty about the smell of the drugstore, the crinkle of the shopping bag, the taste of a new lipstick, the promise of lips transformed—dull before, bold after.

This desire stayed with me, and I fed

it slowly. Lipsticks, then conditioner. Then a blouse, and soon thereafter shoes, jacket, new curtains.

It was this power that I now see we were conjuring, for years, in Los Angeles. It was this power that fueled Ken's late nights in the office, my panic attacks in the kitchen, our stucco townhome, our stucco debt. It was this power that shaped both our schedules and our finances, and it has been said that how you manage both of these things—your calendar and your checkbook—reveals your truest self.

And here is what I want to say, then, about amassing: It is not powerful. It is simply a waste—of space, of time, of earnings. I tell you this as I survey my shoe rack, as I think of the hours spent online, mindlessly clicking, distractedly exploring in an attempt to find power in leather soles.

Power is not to be found there. Joy is not to be found there. Love is not to be found there.

Remove the weight from your wings.

There is a poster that you have likely seen on Pinterest, that I have likely shared on Pinterest. It is from an Australian poet in Brisbane; her name is Erin too.

It reads, "What if I fall? Oh, but my darling, what if you fly?"

This poster was once pinned—the real way—to my office corkboard, on the corner just next to what you'd imagine would be displayed in any office: books, stationery, the cheerful houseplant.

I received it the week before I decided to become a minimalist, the week before I decided to do the work to simplify, to purge, to be changed for good. I received it the week before I loaded dozens of boxes, bins, garbage bags, miscellaneous shoes, and two blenders into the back of my very suburban minivan to take to the very suburban Goodwill.

Remove the weight from your wings.

I gave away the poster. I gave away the books. I gave away the stationery.

All that remains is what I love.

I kept the cheerful houseplant.

When I lived in Los Angeles, I worked for a woman who organized monthly shopping events called sample sales. We invited fashion designers to haul their overstock of last season's clothing to a hotel ballroom we rented, and then we invited hordes of shoppers to buy it all at a major discount.

It was chaos every time. Hundreds of women spilled through the doors in search of

the greatest deal, their next acquisition, the latest fashion. Clothing racks were knocked over, $420 sweaters were wrinkled and balled up into the corners of slapdash dressing rooms, dresses were trampled to shreds.

It was a frenzy. I can think of no other word to explain it.

When you see the world of fashion from this vantage point, you watch the value of clothing diminish. You see an item we perceive to be of great value—the $420 cashmere sweater, the $800 designer dress—at the end of its life cycle, wrinkled and worn, fought over, torn, then discarded.

Once, after a particularly crazy sale, I asked my boss if she ever thought about the hands that made the clothing, about the minds that stitched the seams.

"I can't," she said, picking up a split silk blouse that had been left behind. "It's too depressing."

My rule in the great slow fashion (quality!) versus fast fashion (quantity!) debate is simple: Use what you have. Shop for what you'll use. Take stock of what you have and wear it. Use it.

This is the best way to honor those who have made your clothing.

An aside: You needn't establish rules for

why it may or may not be appropriate to wear, say, yoga pants to the grocery store. Your yoga pants were made by someone. They were designed, they were stitched, they were seamed, they were dyed, they were woven, they were packaged.

Wear them to buy your milk. Wear them wherever you'd like.

Shopping consciously is a high and worthy goal, and there are a great many world-changers working hard to create a more ethical consumer experience for all involved.

But to *shop* consciously, we also must *own* consciously. Purchasing a jacket from a Cambodian market is good, unless it gathers dust in your closet—unworn, unused, unloved.

Buy what you need. Need what you wear. Wear what you buy.

When you get used to buying only what you need, needing only what you wear, and wearing only what you buy, you'll notice two things. First, you'll notice that you are flat out in love with—head over heels for—that denim chambray shirt, the black distressed jeans, the moto boots you wear daily.

The second thing you'll notice is that you hate everything else in your closet.

This is okay. A uniform, much like life, is born not of discovering what you love but of noticing what you *don't* love, discarding the things you find yourself ignoring daily, relegated to the depths of the closet this month, next month, seven months down the road.

A uniform, much like life, is born of the understanding that having more options does not guarantee making better choices.

A uniform, much like life, is born of accepting that we should throw the rules out the window. Perhaps there is no right way to skin a cat, to slice an apple, to stock a closet.

Wear the yoga pants, wear the leather pants, wear the skinny jeans or the distressed jeans or the boyfriend jeans or the cuffed jeans or the wide-leg jeans you found in the throwaway bin at your mother-in-law's garage sale.

Because a uniform is a *you*niform.

18.

PATCH WITH GOLD

I had forgotten that time wasn't fixed like concrete but in fact was fluid as sand, or water. I had forgotten that even misery can end.
—*Joyce Carol Oates*, I Am No One You Know

During a Midwest winter, it turns dark by 6:00 p.m.

It turns even darker by 6:30 p.m., when a fellow blogger tells you what you do not know, what you do not wish to know, what no one wishes to know.

That you are being made fun of in a public forum, on a widely read website. That you are being made fun of in the world's break room.

I have heard of this. I have heard tales of bullies and trolls lurking in closed forums, and I have seen beautiful writers, lovely men and women, brave truth-tellers quietly walk away from their words in the presence of online shaming.

It had not yet happened to me, and so I had not yet understood.

It is human nature to draw conclusions in the face of *if*. It is human nature to create an equation from a variable—What *if* it were to happen to me? What would I say? How would I react?

What would become of me?

What would become of my lion?

What might he do in the face of hyenas?

And then *if* becomes *when*, and you find that your equation is useless. The variable is no longer a variable but a known.

It has happened, and now you get to decide what comes next.

My *when*—the public forum—speaks of many things. My smile is too ugly. My jeans are too ripped. My words are too cliche. My writing is too terrible, my lips are too pursed, my thoughts are too flowery, my intentions are too flawed.

I hate that word. I hate the word *too*.

I call Ken, crying. I am back on the tennis court, but this time there are pointing fingers and echoing laughter and roaring crowds. And this time I cannot blame my unfortunate backswing.

My tennis ability is not in question.

I am. It's me that is in question.

My reactions to Ken are a seesaw: *They are right. They are wrong. They are right. They are wrong.*

They are right, aren't they?

I believe I have now settled on, simply, that they are right and they are wrong, and that it shouldn't matter in the slightest.

But of course it matters in the slightest. Of course it matters in the grandest. It mat-

ters when we are cut from the tennis team, when we fail, when our flaws are found out, when we are revealed as the messed-up, imperfect little beings we are. It matters when our jeans are too ripped.

But don't we want to be the ones to say it? Don't we want to be the first to admit our imperfections, to be the first to spot the spinach in our teeth? As much as I want to write, "Heck with the spinach!" I still pull out my compact for a quick peek before the chocolate cake is served.

I have spent more than thirty years avoiding failure. When I was caught redhanded stealing tiny plastic bears from the preschool classroom, when my teacher called home and my mother checked the overflowing pockets of my white minklike coat to find the stowaways, I blamed my friend Katherine, who was promptly grounded.

"She put them there," I said. "I had no idea."

It was a lie, absolutely, because I had every idea. I had big plans for my miniature acquisitions, which included starring roles in the Tiny Bear Parade, scheduled at 4:00 p.m. in my bedroom later that day.

But it was easier to lie. It was easier to

feign innocence, to let someone else's scorecard be sullied. That's what life is, yes? A giant scorecard? Doesn't God peer from over the clouds with a short sharpened pencil—putt-putt style—marking transgressions, measuring failures?

Another bogey for Katherine, he would say.

Researchers agree that some of the greatest minds of our time have one thing in common: the ability to learn from failure. The ability to see discipline, wrong answers, failed hypotheses as opportunities for growth rather than measures of their abilities.

I do not have this mindset, which is why I am here, thirty years later, still struggling to avoid failure.

The result is a never-ending quest to control the scenarios in which failure, in any form, could arise. I will give my best speech, write my greatest article, cook my loveliest dinner, and if you offer constructive criticism of any sort, I will, on most days, offer you an excuse.

My husband loves this about me.

(There is no font for irony.)

Yesterday, then, a conversation.

Ken: "Did you switch the laundry?"

Erin: "No, I didn't get a chance. I got home from errands later than anticipated,

THIS WEEK'S FAILURES

001. Offer an award-winning passive-aggressive side glance to the woman cracking her gum at the post office.

002. Lie to a friend inviting me to dinner. "We've overscheduled," I say. (This is a half-truth. We are semi-busy this week, but we do have flexibility. It just seems easier to lie than to tell the full truth, which is that I don't like her husband, and also they never serve cheese.)

003. Visit Target—it is snowing, I am bored—and spend $129 on meaninglessness.

004. If you'd like to get your own failures off your chest, you may lay them out here:

_____

_____

_____

_____

and then I turned on the stove to heat up sausage and—"

Ken: "Erin? It's okay if you just forgot."

Erin: "No, I didn't forget! I had a lot going on."

Ken: "You forgot."

Erin: "I did *not!*"

I did.

But I could feel that tiny sharp pencil hovering over the scorecard—*Did she remember to serve her husband today?*—and I couldn't bear the majestic, graphite scrawl of God's handwriting: *No.*

Still my fear of failure—no, my fear of being defined by my failure—morphs simple questions like "Did you switch the laundry?" into giant magnifying glasses, illuminating the decisions that mark my days. When it's time to tally up, how many wrong decisions will I have made? Hundreds? In one day? I am a wretch.

And so I choose a different kind of wretch: the lying kind. The kind who justifies, blames, exaggerates, plays the victim.

If I look like a wretch, I might as well wear a mask.

But I'd given up my mask. I'd packed it away for Goodwill. Hadn't I given up my quest for perfection too? Hadn't I yet learned the beauty of gratitude, joy, peace in any circumstance?

Where there is learning, there is always relearning.

After discovering the blog, after crying to Ken on the phone, after resisting the temptation to write a shame-filled email to the website owners, I try to mask my imperfections in a hundred ways. First, I feel sorry for myself. I feel exposed. I feel bare, left naked without my protective layers. There is nowhere to hide, and I begin to doubt this life of less I'm working toward.

Next, I buy new jeans.

Forget minimalism, I think. Maybe a plus sign is just what I need to feel better. I have not yet felt convinced I should fix my smile, but I do wonder about it on my next trip to the dentist.

I do not yet realize that, without grace, pursuing the slow life is just as exhausting as pursuing the fast one. Without grace, minimalism is another metric for perfection.

WITHOUT GRACE, MINIMALISM IS ANOTHER METRIC FOR PERFECTION.

Chasing slow is still a chase.

My friend Mai once told me about kintsugi, a Japanese tradition in which broken pottery is repaired with a metallic-infused lacquer. *Kintsugi* means "to patch with gold"; in this technique, the potter mends a bowl in delicate, sweeping strokes, taking no care to hide the crack. There are no clear coats, there is no blending, there is no attempt at concealing what has occurred. Instead, the crack is illuminated with gold, with respect, with observance.

And then it is pieced together—not to be made new but to be *changed*.

The break itself is the beauty.

The crack is worthy of gold.

Can you imagine?

Kintsugi celebrates failure in a way I am still learning to do, in a way I am only beginning to understand.

Before failure, we are but bowls.

But after failure? After the bad day, the fight with your husband, the spinach in your teeth?

We have been changed. We have a gilded scar to prove it.

Isn't it beautiful?

Doesn't it shine?

Our culture is prone to concealing what is. We applaud women for making a speedy return to prepregnancy jeans after giving birth. We cover evidence of teenage acne with a thirty-four-dollar BB cream. We have become expert under-the-rug sweepers, in marriage and in work, in parenting and in life.

Under-the-rug sweeping is the default.

I once asked my friend what the secret to kintsugi is. Is it the brush? The application? The adhesive, the gold?

"Nah," she said. "It's just time. When my uncle does it, it can take, like, two months."

I hate the answer *time*. Time, historically, has not been on my side.

We are meant to keep an eye on it.

For how long?

While living in this deep season of subtraction, it occurs to me that I have not fully seen it as subtraction. That's interesting, isn't it? Around me, my Rome is falling. In a span of short years, all has crumbled: family, work, finances, my reputation. How have I not seen this as subtraction? How have I not noticed the obvious?

But time marches on daily, and the dirty dishes filling the sink are made clean. Once, my favorite blouse—a vintage lace tunic from the Alameda flea market—was shredded in my mother-in-law's dryer, and I threw it out with the garbage. It pained me to lay it to rest with banana peels and foil balls. That, I remember noticing.

The day before Ken's father died, I went for take-out burgers. It was Memorial Day, and on principle alone, burgers seemed to be an integral part of a celebration we were, under no circumstances, having. There were hospice nurses flitting about, and morphine and pills and cell phone alarms set to four-hour increments, our day divided by painkiller doses.

No, there was nothing to celebrate here.

But it was Memorial Day, and I could smell the neighbors' barbecue chicken on the grill, and I could see the tomato vines we had planted weeks earlier just beginning to sprout. It seemed insensitive that time would creep forward without our permission, that tomatoes would grow so boldly, so red, in such an obvious manner.

In this environment? How were they sprouting in this environment?

The burgers. They are significant to me because they marked a very real, very decided change in my perspective. A victim of circumstance is not after burgers on Memorial Day. A helpless woman, a hopeless wallower—she is not ordering extra onion rings. She is not remembering the ketchup packets, she is not stuffing paper napkins into a greasy paper bag.

A victim does not make tiny changes to better her life.

A victim does not celebrate a new day.

But I did, and although Ken's father would be dead by 9:00 a.m. the next morning, burgers or not, it seemed the right thing to do.

And this is what I think of when I think of time.

I think of sprouting tomato plants and dying fathers-in-law, and I think of the small choices we make daily. I think of how we can choose to kintsugi our circumstance, of how we can choose to amass or not, of how we can choose to speed up or not, of how we can choose to gather burgers on a sad, cold summer holiday.

Or not.

I have chosen a lot of the right things, and a lot of the wrong ones. I have tried addition—houses and projects and wardrobes and ambitions. And we have tried subtraction—houses and projects and wardrobes and ambitions.

And then I choose multiplication.

I choose a baby.

3

SURRENDER

00

19.

A FAINT PLUS SIGN

I saw the film / I lived the book /
I got the haircut / That's all it took /
But now I know it's going to take /
A little more now I'm awake.
—Belle and Sebastian, "I Took a Long Hard Look"

We had been living a life of minus, of stripping, of less. I gave away floral skirts and pink blazers and the patent pumps that accompanied me to the courthouse for bankruptcy. We gave away the American dream. We gave away Ken's dad. None of it was easy. Subtraction is not simple.

But today, in my guest bathroom with the coordinated striped towels and the fluoride-free toothpaste, subtraction is not here.

There is a faint plus sign on the stick I am holding, and we are going to be a family of three.

"Just have a baby already," Ken's English grandmother had said for years. When we first moved home to the Midwest and the days were slow and quiet, when we were feeling mopey and listless and drained from the fluorescent hospital lights, Ken and I would ride bikes to visit his grandmother for tea and sandwiches served on Spode china. Once, I talked of the panic attacks in Los Angeles, the sadness that used to envelop me. "It's just hormones. Your body wants a baby. Listen to your body! It has a job to do! Let your body do its job!"

As a favored grandmother, she certainly had a vested interest in the arrival of a dimpled, cooing newborn to snuggle and return. But I think what she was getting at, what I think she was saying, is that our body's job is sometimes to let a baby slide right down our birth canal, up and away, wreaking havoc, building anew, and we'll spend the rest of our lives realizing that we cannot stop the sliding away no matter how much we want to.

It's gravity, that's all.

Ken and I have talked of children many times—when will we be ready? will we ever be ready?—and as we turn the corner to thirty and our HGTV.com show is nearly wrapping, it is decided.

We are certainly not ready, but we will start trying for a child, and the reason is simple and not at all simple: we do not want to be eighty-five in an empty room with a fully lit Christmas tree and no children, grandchildren, great-grandchildren to surround it.

We want the gravity.

Pregnancy, for many women, is the great slamming on of the brakes in your life. Others see your comfort and well-being as vital to the baby's comfort and well-being. So for a brief time, your sole purpose is to aid the baby in its survival. Your womb is the car seat, the baby carrier, the bassinet, the blanket, the A/C unit, the food, the water, the love.

For gracious sakes, put your feet up! Get out of the kitchen; we've got the dishes under control. You're resting for two now. Did you take those vitamins yet today?

For me, pregnancy is the first time I

WE LIVE OUR ENTIRE LIVES WITH INHERENT
UNFATHOMABLE VALUE, AND IT TAKES
A WATERMELON UNDER OUR SHIRT FOR
OTHERS TO NOTICE IT. FOR US TO BELIEVE IT.

care for myself holistically. I take daily, mile-long walks to the park and back—*Boost that heart rate; babies love a quick beat!*—I eat my greens—*The more folic acid, the higher the IQ!*—and I take measures to quiet my mind—*Think positively! The baby can sense your stress!*

It's an odd thing. We live our entire lives with inherent unfathomable value, and it takes a watermelon under our shirt for others to notice it. For us to believe it.

For us to do something about it.

7-24-12

Our daughter, Bee, is born in our master bedroom on a hot July night as Bob, the elderly next-door neighbor from Georgia, mows his lawn. I have not yet asked him about the sounds he heard that night. We have not yet made eye contact.

If pregnancy is the great slamming on of the brakes in your life, choosing a home birth is the great slamming on of the brakes in everyone else's life. Choose to have a home birth, and choose to welcome the rub-berneckers in troves; choose to create the relational traffic jam that will follow.

Choose to have a home birth and you will choose to have your childhood best friend's mother contact you via Facebook to

FIVE REACTIONS TO "I'M HAVING A HOME BIRTH"

001. By choice?
002. In front of the dogs?
003. My [insert distant relative] had a home birth. Just right there in the [back yard, truck, cornfield, shed]. The kid just popped right out, and her husband's, like, [insert expletive].
004. If you have the baby in the kitchen, I am *never ever* again coming for brunch.
005. Cool! [Subject change. Weather works well here.]

share of her daughter's recent C-section, how the baby would not—no, could not!—have survived at home. She will beg you to reconsider, for the sake of your life and the life of your daughter. You will have your favorite server at Panera ask if midwives wash their hands before they catch the baby. You will have strangers in the comments section of a popular parenting website question, "What? A water birth? Babies can't swim! What kind of a parent are you going to be?"

You will have friends who roll their eyes at you, who call you a hippie, who dismiss the idea and proclaim epidurals to be an elixir of the gods.

And then you will have friends who are supportive, who would never choose to have their baby next to the vacuum cleaner, the shoe closet, the tax records, but who will smile with their eyes when you tell them you are terrified to become a mother.

That we can all agree on.

Shortly after Bee's birth, gifts begin trickling through our doors. We receive Orla Kiely baby books and tiny little metallic leather moccasins. I open impeccably wrapped pampering sets with lavender belly balms and peppermint bath salts. One friend sends a tube of La Mer concealer and a bag of fair trade coffee—"The True Mama Essentials!" the card reads.

One package arrives in a flat mailer, and we don't notice it for days. Ken brought it in from the mail while I was on a grocery run and left it on the kitchen counter. (You know the thing about kitchen counters. They're like Vegas. What happens there stays there, until you search for your gynecologist's business card in a mountain of roast beef coupons and Restoration Hardware catalogs and you sweep it all into the kitchen trash, craps style.)

"Did you open your package from Shannon?" he asks later that week over leftover lasagna. (My wedding shower advice has proved true. It seems everyone does, indeed, have two lasagnas in their freezer—one for births—and we are the grateful recipients of seven? eight? varieties.)

"What package?" I ask, biting into a reheated slice of garlic bread. Garlic bread is never any good the second time around.

"It's over on the counter," Ken says. "But be quiet! Don't wake her." Bee is a fussy sleeper from the start, and we've grown accustomed to chewing quietly, blinking quietly, breathing quietly.

I tiptoe to the kitchen. Shannon is one of my favorite people, an old soul wrapped in tanned skin. She wears vintage aprons when she makes waffles for her kids, her brunette hair in loose waves sometimes catching the batter. She uses the fine china not to impress anyone but because she likes the sound her fork makes against the delicate bone. "Plus, it makes my eggs look so pretty in the morning," she says. She offers agave for your tea. She writes in cursive. She paints sunsets on Thursday afternoons.

She is small and unassuming, but then you'll hear her belting a Sara Bareilles song in the car and you'll wonder how her tiny frame could hold such a big voice.

I find her package under a borrowed copy of *The Baby Whisperer* and I sneak into the bedroom to tear the mailer open as loudly as I'd like. A small box with a scrawled note falls onto the unmade bed.

Dear Erin,

You tried to give this away years ago during your purging phase, but I kept it for you. I thought you might have a daughter someday, and I thought she'd like to have it.

XOXO

In the small box, wrapped in tissue paper that smells of Shannon's kitchen, of waffles and chai, I see my wedding necklace.

I remember the night I put it in the giveaway stack. I told her I'd never liked it much, that I'd bought it at Claire's in the mall a few days before the wedding, that it was the only necklace I could find that matched an ivory dress. Do you know how hard it is to match ivory? How hard it is *not* to match white? It seems there are a million shades between.

I hadn't seen Shannon rescue it from the giveaway stack that night. I hadn't seen her take it, put it in the pocket of her Free People poncho, and store it in her midcentury sideboard for the next five? six? seven? years. I hadn't seen her stumble on it sometimes, when looking for an extra place setting for

guests or for the olivewood bowl she likes to serve her strawberry poppy-seed salad in.

"I thought you might have a daughter someday," the card read.

I hadn't thought of that.

"And I thought she'd like to have it."

I hadn't thought of that either.

After Bee arrives, every plant in our house withers, yellows, and dies within the week. It is not for lack of water or love, or at least I don't think it is. Perhaps they simply feel the neglect, the shift in attention, the reorganized hierarchy of life.

But maybe it is me? What do I know about keeping something alive? How can I know how much water is too much water, how little sunlight is too little sunlight?

What do I know of enough?

When I was a child, my favorite Barbie was run over by my uncle's pickup truck on some average summer day. I was careless, and I left Ms. Indiana on the driveway after a vigorous round of eveningwear competition. I was in search of vanilla wafers in the kitchen, that is all.

But moments later while pouring a glass of milk, I heard the sound of gravel churning under rubber tires, and in an instant of flattening plastic and scattering Barbie heels, any faith I'd had in my mothering abilities was smashed.

She was, and then she wasn't.

I had known better. I had seen *Rescue 911*, after all, and I knew it takes just one moment of averting your eyes, just one mistake, just one misstep—just one vanilla wafer—to change the course of a child's life. To flatten a Barbie, or worse.

And it is only a plastic memory, but Bee isn't plastic—she is 60 percent Ken and 40 percent me, and all of our houseplants have died and how can something so small, so light, feel so heavy in my arms?

And I suppose it is these thoughts that cause the tremors in me now, when I look down at the newborn baby who has finished her milk, and her eyelids are fluttering, and she is at peace, and I am an earthquake.

No one ever told me how much fear is hidden in love.

 NO ONE EVER TOLD ME HOW MUCH
FEAR IS HIDDEN IN LOVE.

OO

20.

*You know how I always seem to be struggling,
even when the situation doesn't call for it?*
—*Carrie Fisher,* Postcards from the Edge

My friends from Los Angeles email. They'll be in the Midwest for a few days; could they detour on their road trip to come and take photos of the baby?

It is Tuesday, and I'm sneaking in a rare morning of updating the blog while Ken puts two-month-old Bee down for an early nap. I peek over my laptop and survey the state of my home office. A room that was once splashed across the glossy front page of HGTV.com—all layered sheepskins and designer floor lamp—is now unrecognizable. Yesterday, the dog threw up a chewed diaper and the clean-up towel is still tossed aside in the corner, crusted with vomit. A stack of unwritten thank-you notes and needs-to-be-thrown-away paperwork sits on my desk, paperweighted by three half-empty coffee mugs and a bottle of hot sauce (?). A towering baby swing with dancing elephants is pushed to the side, next to the unfolded laundry pile with monkey onesies, Bee's lion blanket, the pig bib.

A zoo, I think.

I return to my email and begin typing an excuse that is both believable and glamorous. "I'm so sorry," I begin. "We're thinking of celebrating Bee's two-month birthday with a trip to the lake . . ."

My words are interrupted by Bee's dinosaur screams from the nursery. She is frantic. Ken is attempting to rock her, to quiet her, and her face is reddening with anger. "Can you try feeding her again?" Ken asks.

"I just fed her! I am working! I need to work!" and I realize that I have pronounced *work* as if it were a curse word, as if it were a gun and it is loaded and I have shot him in the heart.

Because our move to the Midwest didn't come with a job for Ken—not many Hollywood filmmakers need feature editors roaming the lemonade-stand suburban streets of Indiana—Ken is not only mourning the loss of his father, he is also mourning the loss of a career he loves. I have been selfish and unsympathetic and preoccupied, and it was only a matter of time before the resentment surfaced, before the bullet pierced.

This is the first and only time Ken leaves the house in a fury, the front door slamming so hard that I'm sure I see our entryway sign— "All Are Welcome"—rattle. He is a picture of patience, of kindness, a master of conflict resolution, and I have broken him and he has left.

He is gone for forty-five minutes, and it is enough. Bee is calm now, and I adjust her swaddle and move to the living room sofa, where I look at her face and apologize for the yelling. I feel angry and overworked and resentful and uprooted and tired from learning and relearning this motherhood game, but there is something else, something deeper that I cannot identify.

I feel scared.

I am scared, is all.

I look at Bee, a budding plant, and I wonder if this marriage bed can nourish her growth. Are we strong enough to hold her, to keep her, to fight for her and with her and over her without shooting bullets at each other?

I am not asking myself. I am asking God.

A hot tear leaves my eye and enters hers as she lies swaddled on my lap. She blinks reflexively and I want nothing more than to rewind the day, to change my tone, to choose a different morning to work, but I am relieved it has surfaced. Fish are far less frightening swimming near the surface than they seem lurking in the deep below.

Ken returns as I wipe the last of my tears, as Bee falls asleep on my chest. He says some terrible things and I say a few more terrible things, and then he says one tiny-bit-lovely thing and I say one more tiny-bit-lovely thing, and here the healing begins. We are working toward lovely again.

When I was pregnant with Bee, a girlfriend offered this advice: Do not bring up anything important, if you can help it, until the baby is six months old. It will not end well.

"Sleep deprivation always wants the last word," she said.

And it is the sleep deprivation, partly, that loaded my gun that morning, but the gun has always been loaded, hasn't it?

We are lucky. The wound isn't devastating. We have survived, and likely we will heal without irreparable damage.

And we have told the truth. I have finally told the truth that I've known but could not yet admit, that we are but fragile creatures, every last one of us.

That, on most days, we're not perfect, but we're fine, and on some days, we're not fine, but we're okay, and on a few singular days of the year: nothing is okay, not even a little, and everything is terrible, and forever, amen.

And that this fragility, this delicate nature of being, is the life we're commissioned to celebrate.

ACCEPTABLE MESSES FOR YOUR FRIENDS TO SEE

001. Your laundry mountain, at its worst.
002. Your junk mail pile, at its worst.
003. Your unwashed hair, at its worst.
004. Your parenting mistakes, at their worst.
005. You, at your worst.

FALL 2012

A few days later, while Bee is gently rocking in her elephant swing, I draft a new email to our LA friends.

"Yes, please come visit our zoo. We could use some fresh air, if you don't mind the dust bunnies."

The leaves are just beginning to chatter when my friends arrive on a cool September afternoon. Ken and I have spent the morning vacuuming coffee grinds from tile grout and ironing the sheets. We haven't yet learned a key tenet of hospitality: Leave the mess; they're not coming to see your toilets.

Our friends have hit traffic and are an hour late, so I begin my habit of counting down the minutes to my next nursing session, Bee's next nap, her diaper change prior, and I tally up the time available between— maybe a half hour?

I never knew how much math is required of a new mother.

We usher our friends into the kitchen for pistachios and tea, and Ken gives me a look that reminds me to relax, to forget the schedule, to stop counting minutes in my head.

I try, I do.

I fail.

Ken is heating the kettle and entertaining our friends with stories of mothers-in-law as my mind drifts to the clock, to the running list of variables I have come to predict in a feeble attempt to control the outcries of a newborn. I am rigid. I believe motherhood can be figured out, that taking care of newborns is simply a matter of routine, of expectation. It's a science, a formula. There is no room for veering.

I laugh heartily and interject when I can, but I am not following this conversation; I am following the one in my mind. *It has been forty minutes. Has she wet her diaper? Should I feed her before the photos, or after? Maybe I should warm a bottle now, pump later? Ken can give her a bottle; I can relax. No, no, I need to nurse. It is hot. Is my hair getting frizzy? Is Bee as hot as I am?*

Bee fusses and I glance at the clock to see it is feeding time, but our friends are readying their cameras—"Can we snap a few now? The light is perfect."

I feign flexibility—"Sure!"—as we head to the sunroom, and Bee quiets as we wave wooden toys in her face and wait for giggles. She is happy to enjoy a change of scenery. I am still—always, ever—glancing at the clock, hyperaware of the time, readjusting the schedule in fifteen-minute intervals.

There is a photo from that day, from those few minutes in the sunroom, and in it I am looking at the camera with Bee in my arms. A smile is plastered on my face, but my eyes reveal fear. My eyes have given me away.

My smile, toothy and wide, tells tales of baby bliss—of nursery rhymes and bubble baths and mother-daughter bonds. *Just look at us*, it says. *We are a portrait of happiness.*

But my eyes. My eyes are narrowed, distant, cloudy. They whisper secrets of anxiety, of fears faced and the ones to come. My eyes will widen the time Bee splits her lip on a toy chest, they will witness her first allergic reaction to a cleaning solution, they will continue to betray the deep insecurity I feel, the quest for control, the desire for perfection.

My smile is a liar.

My eyes are a mother.

As our friends finish their photo shoot, I excuse myself to the nursery to

MATH LESSON 009 // PISTACHIO SHELLS + ULTRAFINE SHARPIE = PISTACHIO FAMILY PORTRAIT (YOUR KID WILL LOVE THIS)

feed Bee. She has grown fussy again, and I blame myself, but not entirely. Something has shifted. The schedule has veered and the world has not ended.

Can this be motherhood also?

Later, Ken and I take turns brushing our teeth as we recap the day. "You missed a great afternoon," he jokes.

"I know," I say.

I used to think the opposite of control is chaos. But it's not.

The opposite of control is surrender.

 I USED TO THINK THE OPPOSITE OF CONTROL IS CHAOS. BUT IT'S NOT. THE OPPOSITE OF CONTROL IS SURRENDER.

OO

21.

THERE'S NO
SECRET, HONEY

And what did you want? To call myself beloved,
to feel myself beloved on the earth.
—Raymond Carver, "Late Fragment"

Surrendering control is, of course, the easy part.

Surrendering expectation is more muddied.

When I first purged my belongings, when I first saw the beauty in a minimalist lifestyle, in the art of subtraction, I culled mounds of gently used clothing from my wardrobe. A friend who worked with a women's shelter in Colorado once told me that the bulk of the items they usually received were stained, torn, or in poor shape. The women had nothing to wear for job interviews.

I can help, I thought, and I gathered six boxes to fill during the next few days.

I spend a morning carefully folding gently used cashmere sweaters and getting old heels resoled by the downtown cobbler. I iron dozens of button-up blouses and steam dresses that still hold their tags. I place layers of tissue paper between slacks; I line each box with scented drawer inserts. I write handwritten notes of encouragement for each package and make two trips to the post office to ship them all the next week.

A month later, I email my friend. "Did you receive the boxes? Just want to be sure!"

I don't, of course, just want to be sure. I want a proper thank-you. I want a return on my investment, an acknowledgment of my service. I want praise in exchange for my good deed. A gold star, please.

She responds, after four days, with a "Got it—thanks!"

I have not since donated clothing to her shelter, and I am not proud of this fact.

When we serve from this place, from a place of expectation, of mutual back-scratching, of deeds for praise, it is not true service. When we decide that "Got it—thanks" does not properly reflect the effort we have put into an act of service, this is not a place of true sacrifice.

Points, tallies, scores—these matter only in Scrabble. We don't get to amass gold stars for choosing minimalism, for cleaning the toilets, for saving the whales.

And yet this is the place from which I have served my marriage for ten years now. This is the place from which I encouraged Ken to take a snowboarding retreat when Bee was an infant (he'll return the favor someday), from which I scrubbed the kitchen oven (he'll thank me when he gets home), from which I spent hours on a stationary bike at the gym (he'll praise my calves).

And when these things don't happen, when the praise does not reflect the amount of effort I have put into the service, I get busy tallying my scorecard. Dishes, two points. Laundry, four. Monday night trash duty? Three points in the summer; eight in a cold, dark winter.

And this is where I am on a Tuesday when I'm finding it difficult to pick Ken's socks up off the floor without a resentful *tsk-tsk* in my mind.

The expectation in marriage is that the score should be even. An equal partnership.

POINTS, TALLIES, SCORES—THESE MATTER ONLY IN SCRABBLE. WE DON'T GET TO AMASS GOLD STARS FOR CHOOSING MINIMALISM, FOR CLEANING THE TOILETS, FOR SAVING THE WHALES.

Fifty-fifty. His and hers, like my mother's monogrammed hand towels. And when it is not, I scale back my service—*Oh, those socks? I didn't even see them!*—so he can feel the weight of my disappointment.

Of course, a scorecard has nothing to do with service or sacrifice or even love. It has to do with control. It is about manipulation. It is math: I'll scratch your back, and I'll let you know when I am angered that you didn't offer to scratch mine.

In the Bible, this is said:

"Freely you have received; freely give" (Matt. 10:8).

Maybe love isn't really a two-way street. Maybe there's nothing fifty-fifty about it. Maybe, instead, love is a bit like candy in a parade or a pinata or a backyard Easter egg hunt. There's enough to go around; it needn't be rationed. No math required.

I once believed there is little room for empowerment in a marriage. I watched working women in suit jackets and pumps on Monday mornings, fighting glass ceilings, chasing corner offices, bloodying their cuticles during the week and covering the scars with a coat of fresh nail polish on the weekend. I wondered what it was like for their husbands. Were they proud? Jealous? Did they no longer feel necessary in the partnership? Did they feel pushed aside, reprioritized, lower on the totem pole of female actualization?

If we could have it all—big, whole, full lives—what would that mean for our other halves?

How much room is left for them?

We are six women, all sprawled on terry cloth towels by a pool in Palm Springs. Our families—kids, dogs, husbands, friends—are thousands of miles away. We have gathered to celebrate the anniversary of a successful project; among us are acclaimed authors, PR experts, food stylists, and fashion mavens. Empowerment radiates from every fiber of our black, high-waisted swimsuits.

And here we are, sipping on mojitos in sun hats, talking about men.

When the topic arrives, when we ask ourselves what the secret to a happy marriage might be, our theories are few. It's anyone's guess, after all.

But then my friend tells us what her grandmother had whispered to her, lavender bouquet in hand, at her grandparents' fiftieth anniversary party. "There's no secret, honey," she confessed. "We just never fell out of love at the same time."

That's it.

There is another way, of course. It is not foolproof or guaranteed—nothing ever is—and yet it holds promise beyond sheer luck and good timing. It offers another shade to the muddy brown mix of work and commitment, to the daily decision to recommit, to fall back in love, to pray your spouse offers the same each day.

It is, simply, sacrifice.

Culturally, we are taught many things about relationships. We are taught that love is magnetic, a force field, and that to be desirable, we must attract and not polarize.

The attracting is easy, of course. We must work hard (*spin class at 5:00 p.m.!*), build ourselves up (*hair appointment next Tuesday!*), become self-actualized (*don't forget book club tonight!*).

But the part where we're taught not to polarize? To smile and nod? Quiet your emotions? Swallow hard? Do not, under any circumstances, say what you *actually* think?

There is danger in this.

We think our formula will produce positive results. That after the attracting (the

A FEW SECRETS TO A HAPPY MARRIAGE

001. Never turn down a romp in the hay.
002. Don't nag him about golf.
003. Act interested, even when he brings up *Battlestar Galactica*.
004. Agree to disagree, in life and in menus.

YOUR TURN?

_____

_____

_____

_____

_____

THE ANSWER TO A HAPPY MARRIAGE IS THE SAME
AS THE ANSWER TO A HAPPY LIFE. IT IS SIMPLE,
AND IT IS NOT AT ALL SIMPLE: GIVE FREELY.

cut, the color), the not polarizing (the smile, the nod), surely love will find us. Love will notice us. Love will see our glory. How could it not? Look at us; we shine. (Brighter than kintsugi, even.)

There was a time when I believed this to be true.

But on the bad days, the days when the dishes are piled and the washing machine has broken and *Did you make the bank transfer—wait, you said you would!* and the kids have brought in a dead mouse from the back yard, it's easy to fall out of love at the same time. It's easy to see the fault in our formula. It's easy to look at the person across the dinner table, to study their face, to look at their fading youth, the muted freckles, to see a stranger who asks too much of you, who cannot see your shine.

Maybe my friend's grandmother is right, I think as we towel off and slurp the last of the mojitos, chewing the basil stems, willing the moon to stay high, to prolong our getaway.

Maybe a successful marriage means just never falling out of love at the same time.

But I'm not convinced that's all there is to it.

My brother-in-law, an architect, once told me that a key tenet in design and construction is that a building is only as strong as it is soft. "It takes a very real amount of flexibility," he said. "We think it's about weight, about power, but it's not really at all. It's gotta be soft."

It is impossible to serve continually, to give freely, to sacrifice fully without power. Without strength and focus, without forbearance. It takes strength to pick up his socks from the floor, softness not to mention he should know better.

Maybe it's not about being empowered at all, whether we are or whether we are not. Maybe it's about what we do with our empowerment.

It came quickly, like our Palm Springs sunburns, this realization that I had been approaching marriage the wrong way for nearly ten years. It was a rare moment, a jolt, a neon sign. How often do we get a neon sign, with a mojito no less?

The answer to a happy marriage cannot be based on luck, on timing. On empowerment alone. On our ability to spotlight the parts of ourselves that attract, on our ability to hide the parts of ourselves that don't. On our ability to keep ourselves from falling out of love at the same time.

No, the answer to a happy marriage is the same as the answer to a happy life.

It is simple, and it is not at all simple: Give freely.

That's it. That is everything and that is nothing, and it is the best we can offer; it is the best we can do. Give freely. Pick up the socks. Take out the trash. Let him sleep in. Get the oil changed (*but that's his job!*), and get the oil changed again and again and again.

I no longer believe that love, like candy in a parade, is wasted if it falls through the cracks. Service doesn't require a willing recipient.

Love doesn't either, not really.

But it does require great power.

And we have been given it.

"Freely you have received; freely give" (Matt. 10:8).

By the way. Do you know who is having the most fun at the parades? Do you know who is granted the biggest smile?

It is she who is throwing the candy, of course.

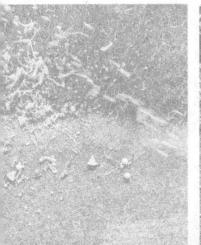
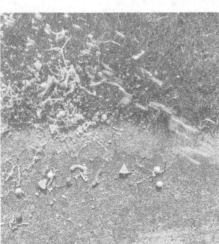

22.

WILL THERE EVER BE TULIPS?

Am I supposed to do something important? /
It doesn't seem enough / to merely take up space /
on this planet / in this country /
in this state / in this town / in this family.
—*Sharon Creech,* Heartbeat

I'm often asked for advice on decorating. How can I offer symmetry in an asymmetrical living room? How can I make the most of my tiny kitchen? Where can I store our winter coats and hats creatively? And one of my favorites: How can I design the perfect kids' space?

The only answer to this question, in my mind, is never to hang a mirror in a nursery.

When it is 2:00 a.m., when you have not slept in four days, when the baby is shrieking and you are thinking of nipple confusion, you do not want to see your reflection.

Identity is a powerful force. We rarely see ourselves as others do, and we often view the world—our own, someone else's—through a distorted lens.

Every now and then, after a midnight nursing session with Bee, I'd tiptoe out to the kitchen for a glass of water or a handful of chocolate-covered pretzels and I'd sometimes shut the fridge and catch my reflection in the window. *Who is this woman with the dark circles, the bedhead?* I'd wonder. *Who am I, now that I am not my own? Who will I become, now that I am divided?*

It was Mother's Day, and Bee was not yet one. At church I looked around the carpeted sanctuary to see hundreds of mothers beaming in their floral midi skirts and striped flats. Their purses held hand-drawn cards decorated with stickers, their necks bore gifts of jewelry that held the stamped initials of each of their children, one-two-three, in rose gold, please. Their smiles held love, pride, confidence.

I believe that is the word for what I saw deepest on their red-painted lips. I believe it is called confidence.

As a new mother, it was not confidence that I felt. I was not confident that Bee would love me the way I loved her or that she would on some Mother's Day present me with a doodled doily, a breakfast of toast, a tulip from the garden.

It did not seem a reality I was equipped to imagine. Just that morning,

Bee had accidentally torn out a chunk of my hair, and I'd screamed at her.

There had been no tulips.

Would there ever be tulips?

And this is the first moment it occurred to me that if I could not be a good mother, if there was the slightest possibility that love would not be returned to me in the form of finger-paint drawings and admiration, then perhaps I could spare some love elsewhere. If I could not guarantee success at motherhood, I could guarantee success at work.

I do not have to tell you, then, that my return to the world of more was fueled not by my passion to work but by my passion to avoid failure.

It began innocently enough. I had been feeling creatively starved, ready for a new project, and when Bee began sleeping through the night, I'd heat the kettle and work until 2:00 a.m. launching a new project—the ultimate women's lifestyle destination online. I went on to hire a staff of eleven reporting from nearly every major city in the United States. Collectively, our

reach spanned fourteen million women and we published daily articles on topics we were individually passionate about, from concealer to cancer, from music to the mundane.

I loved the work. I did. I was proud of the launch, of the press, of the praise from loyal readers who had grown to appreciate the site as a valuable roadmap to life.

It hadn't occurred to me that when you offer a roadmap to another, you no longer have your own. That if you don't know your whereabouts by heart, you risk losing yourself in a great big and beautiful world.

This is how it starts when you add more than you were intended to add. You grow confused, a bit lost, and you think the answer might be that you're not working hard enough. That you need to add more. More hours, more 2:00 a.m. coffee, more photo shoots, bigger budgets, more staff members, more editorial retreats, more sponsorship packages, more readers and followers and

Tweets and pings and conference calls and press interviews.

So I did. I added more. I added in the spirit of hard work, in the spirit of sharing the message, in the spirit of attaining the perfection I had so wanted to attain in motherhood alone.

It is the tennis courts again and the finger-pointing and the spilled rice. It is the breakdowns, the bankruptcy, the many failures that I didn't have the strength to kintsugi.

This is what I'm thinking of.

Motherhood is hard in a way I am ill-equipped for, in the way that you must learn to sweep cereal bits off the floor without sweeping your own self right out the door with them. There is the crying, from you and the baby, and the learning, by you and the baby, and the growing, of you and the baby.

It is an emptying like none I have felt before—the nursing, the lack of sleep, the surveying of her every cough, gasp, gurgle. And it is a filling like none I have felt—the first smile, a quizzical staredown, an eventual giggle.

But for a long time, for those first few months, it was mostly emptying.

I suppose that's where the love fits in.

As it is with any empty space, with any leftover room—whether a side porch or a heart chamber—either you can let it be, or you can fill it up.

For nearly two years, I push through the tension. I ignore the signs that I am overworked, that I am distracted, that I have been moving too quickly through life in an attempt to chase something other than what I have already been given.

I am chasing a new identity—that of a working mother who has achieved a perfect balance. More spills from every corner of my life. I am the driving force, ramping up the speed. It is me, behind the wheel, accelerating, pedal to the metal, rarely checking the rearview mirror to see all I'm leaving behind.

Speed, of course, is helpful when searching for something. You'll get there faster, and in the great hunt for my identity, I want to get there faster. I want a shortcut.

HOW TO FILL AN EMPTY SPACE

001. Start a new project. I launched a website, but a kitchen remodel will do, sometimes a baby.

002. Throw a dinner party for twelve. Say, "No gifts, please!" (You will get six bottles of wine.)

003. Buy more toys. That miniature wooden kitchen would look great in the sunroom, and those pans are on sale. Wait, tiny felt bananas? Add to cart, add to cart, add to cart.

004. Get a plant. Fiddle leaf figs are all the rage, and nearly indestructible, right?

005. Brush up on your celebrity gossip. Contemplate the meaning of life in Justin Bieber lyrics. Begin to understand the Kardashians.

006. Forget to water the fiddle leaf fig tree.

007. Hire a housekeeper.

008. Take on the promotion at work. Buy that new oxblood handbag your colleague loves. Iron your skirt. Tame the flyaways. Look the part.

009. Replace the fiddle leaf fig tree with six succulents. Much hardier.

010. Reschedule last week's playdate.

011. Get a new haircut, new lipstick, etc. You'll have whatever Alexa Chung is having.

012. Retire that new oxblood handbag. Buy the pebbled leather version instead, the one on Refinery29, the one large enough to fit "all your selves."

013. Rearrange the sunroom. Move the wooden kitchen, the pans, the tiny bananas into storage. You've had your eye on a Hans Wegner chair.

HOW TO EMPTY A SPACE

001. Ignore the signs.
002. Distract yourself.
003. Push forward.
004. Pull through.
005. Break down.

WHAT HAVE YOU TRIED?

_____

_____

_____

_____

I have been given a family. I have been given the gift of motherhood. I have been given a husband who offers immense support. I have been given a job, my own humble lifestyle blog that has sustained us for years, that could continue to sustain us, could continue to offer enough.

But I add more to the equation.

During my season of overworking, of pursuing productivity over peace, I often bring takeout home after a long stretch of work at the coffee shop. (It never occurs to me that I am likely spending any excess income from this massive project on takeaway pasta and Chinese delivery to feed my family the food I am too busy to prepare at home.)

Once, after a particularly frenzied day of a missed deadline, a botched article, and a slew of technical programming errors, I walk into Jimmy John's to grab sub sandwiches for Ken. Bee is already in bed—I've missed reading to her, again. I've missed so many things in the past few months especially—her first friend's birthday party, her first trip to the zoo, her first haircut.

It's not that I have been absent. We've had a simple morning routine together, waking up with the sun, making eggs, dancing to the Tarzan song with the morning light streaming through the kitchen. Our time together is slow, simple—dare I say perfect? But at noon, I need to flip the switch, and so I sometimes watch the clock, my mind growing frenetic as I brace myself for the emails that have stockpiled while I've been . . . what do I call it, our time together in the mornings? The emails that have stockpiled while I've been gone? While I've been distracted? Distracted from what, exactly? From work?

Surely it is meant to be the other way around.

Still, I work long afternoons at the coffee shop, attempting to multitask, to squeeze every minute of productivity to make up for the hours I am not working. I've thrown myself into a full-time job with only part-time hours available, and I have a team of eleven relying on me to lead by example.

This is not the example I intended. This is not the precedent I want to set.

But this is where I am, at Jimmy John's, on a familar evening, waiting for a number 6 and a number 12, no cheese.

I scan the artwork on the walls,

the quirky signs, the humorous slogans—"Bread so French it must be liberated!"—and stumble upon this poster, titled "The Mexican Fisherman":

The American investment banker was at the pier of a small coastal Mexican village when a small boat with just one fisherman docked. Inside the small boat were several large fin tuna. The American complimented the Mexican on the quality of his fish and asked how long it took to catch them.

The Mexican replied, "Only a little while."

The American then asked why he didn't stay out longer and catch more fish.

The Mexican said he had enough to support his family's immediate needs.

The American then asked, "But what do you do with the rest of your time?"

The Mexican fisherman said, "I sleep late, fish a little, play with my children, take siesta with my wife, Maria, stroll into the village each evening where I sip wine and play guitar with my amigos. I have a full and busy life."

The American scoffed. "I am a Harvard MBA and could help you. You should spend more time fishing and with the proceeds, buy a bigger boat, and with the proceeds from the bigger boat you could buy several boats. Eventually, you would have a fleet of fishing boats. Instead of selling your catch to a middleman, you would sell directly to the processor, eventually opening your own cannery. You would control the product, processing, and distribution. You would need to leave this small coastal fishing village and move to Mexico City, then LA, and eventually NYC, where you will run your expanding enterprise."

The Mexican fisherman asked, "But how long will this take?"

To which the American replied, "Fifteen to twenty years."

"But what then?"

The American laughed and said that's the best part. "When the time is right, you would announce an IPO and sell your company stock to the public and become very rich; you would make millions."

"Millions?" asked the fisherman. "Then what?"

The American said, "Then you would retire. Move to a small coastal fishing village where you would sleep late, fish a little, play with your kids, take siesta with your wife, stroll to the village in the evening, sip wine, and play guitar with your amigos!"

—*Author unknown*

"Number 6, number 12?" the sandwich maker calls. I blink and walk slowly to the counter. I thank him, for more than the subs.

Later that night, I drive home with a crinkly bag of sandwiches and sneak in through the garage—*Shh! She's sleeping!*—and put the subs on the counter and my laptop bag on the floor, and I ask Ken if we can sell the website, if we can get back to the way things were, if I can go back to my small, humble blog that made us an adequate living, that offered us everything we needed, and if we can forget the rest.

"Can we survive without it?" I ask him.

"Can we survive *with* it?" he asks me.

I sell the website in the next six months, and we slow our lives tremendously. I write in the mornings because I love to, not because I have three deadlines in the afternoon. I work for a few hours, take a yoga class, walk in the door by noon to spend an hour or two singing "Itsy Bitsy Spider," changing diapers, offering baths, chopping strawberries, soaking cashews for a new dinner recipe. We adventure in the afternoons—just Bee and me—and Ken starts projects of his own. We have margin. We have space. We have room for ourselves, for others.

It is the life I've always wanted, with fewer dollar signs to our name.

It is sleeping late, playing with our child, taking siesta with my husband, strolling to the village in the evening, sipping wine, and playing guitar with my amigos.

I would love to tell you that there were no casualties as a result of my behavior, but there were many. I will not gain back the months of tension, of stress, of regrets, and I can only now accept them as the clumsy patching of my own pottery.

I can only now paint the next cracks gold.

23.

POOR, LOWLY, PLAIN

Life is a quest to find an unfindable thing.
We are put here needing something that doesn't exist here.
—*Glennon Doyle Melton,* Carry On, Warrior

I suppose you need to clean out your garage on a sunny, 73 degree afternoon one time and one time only to fully realize the truth as you know it, the truth made evident as you wade knee-deep in a creek of rusted can openers, cracked patio chairs, frayed sweaters piled high.

There is so much here.

I'd purged my closet. I'd simplified my life. But there is always more work to be done. It is an ongoing process, isn't it?

Here, in my garage, I am floating amid cardboard boxes toppling over with things I have collected, with excess I have amassed from years of indecision and impatience, wrong choices and impulsive emotions.

To my left, a used crock pot. It is red, ceramic, and rusted, and it whispers of the moment months prior when I'd replaced it—an upgrade, I believe we have labeled this—with a shiny, stainless version. The stainless crock pot is larger, and I'd "needed" larger, and I must stop this story here, I must stop writing this to tell you that I will no longer be placing quotation marks around the words *needed* and *needs* and *need*, but can

I trust you to place them there for me? Can I trust you to join me in the understanding that we need so little, truly, and certainly not multiple crock pots?

I will go on.

To my right, a towering fire pit my husband and I acquired that one spring in LA, our minds aflurry with visions of al fresco dinners on our balcony under a starry sky. But it takes time to build a fire, and commitment to relax around it, and after all, the lawn needed mowing—did you add quotation marks?—and the mosquitoes were out, and tomorrow, we say. Tomorrow we'll have a fire.

And now it has rusted. How many times had we built a fire? Six? Maybe seven?

There is so much here.

And in the corner, the far left corner, four bags of black mulch, floral-lined gloves, a trowel. Gardening plans had been on the agenda. I remember this phase well. I was thirsty after a particularly dry season and a friend suggested gardening, a hobby. "It's easy," she promised, and so a few days later, there I was in the garden section of our home improvement store, asking after hyacinths and hostas, calendulas and chrysanthemums, plants I could not yet spell the names of but certainly could care for, surely yes. I

was to be a gardener, after all; this was to be my hobby. This was to fill my void, to be my purpose, my completion.

It was, in the end, not to be, and instead, I spent that sad spring in bed quite a lot, a dog on either side, a pile of unread books on the nightstand, the trowel unused in the far left corner of our garage.

In front of me are the bins, the endless bins that hold chipped Christmas decorations meant to bring joy, clothing meant to bring comfort, books meant to bring inspiration. And sometimes, they do.

Most times they gather dust and require some sort of maintenance, and now, here we are, here I am, cleaning out the garage on a sunny, 73 degree afternoon in Indiana, only now it has reached evening and my shoulders are cold.

There is so much here.

There is the baby swing I bought to soothe Bee (I wasn't good enough to do it myself), there is the mandoline slicer I bought to chop things in the kitchen (I wasn't fast enough to do it myself), there is the *Guitar 101* book I bought to learn a new skill (but I wasn't musical enough to do it myself).

A cluttered garage is little more than a graveyard of insecurities, a cemetery of might have been or could have been or should have been.

Or should never have been.

As I shuffle papers resting on a cobweb-covered bookshelf in a garage corner, I stumble upon a newspaper clipping from a year ago. It is from the *New York Times*, and there is my face—flattened, in various hues of smudged black and white and gray. I am smiling, sitting crosslegged in my sunroom on the front page of a section titled "When Blogging Becomes a Slog."

I had been blogging for more than a decade and was interviewed for my contributions, was spotlighted for my slower way of life in the Midwest. For my wise perspective. For my agreeable pace.

Over the years, blogging has become an ever-saturated market. Those of us who began years ago have grown up. We are a decade older. We are a decade wiser.

We are growing tired.

Some of us surrendered, allowing a new crop of bloggers with boundless energy to bloom in our place. Others planted their feet firmly and staked their claim, eyes stretched to the sun while their relationships, peace, and contentment withered in infertile soil.

I chose neither. I chose both. I am the poster girl of in-between, the decision that makes itself for you. But one can straddle the fence only so long.

And now I am in my garage, holding a newspaper known for its accuracy, its truth-telling, its world-class standards. And it praised my slower manifesto, my sustainable career path.

Did they know of the crock pot? Did they peer into my garage and see remnants of a woman who has struggled so much to keep up with the enviable Jones.com? Did they know how many words I spent encouraging bloggers, women, humans to slow down while I sat at the corner table in the coffee shop and missed my baby's first steps?

Did the *New York Times* know how fast I was running to become slow?

I look down at my smiling face, my blonde cropped bob, sitting on a perfectly styled ottoman I acquired during my HGTV .com show. If I squint at the photo, I can see my eucalyptus leaf planter just behind me.

If I squint at the photo, I can see a hypocrite.

On a snowy morning, in my fleece-lined slippers with a hot mug of coffee nearby, I hit "publish" on a blog post that causes ripples within the blogging community and, later, after an interview with the *New York Times*, the world at large.

Its title: "The Rebirth of Slow Blogging."

I could have called it "The Rebirth of Slow Anything," really, because the age-old concept applies to any career, from the phlebotomist to the auto mechanic. We have all, from time to time, chosen the religion of more. Aren't we tired of genuflecting?

Since Bee's birth, since my fear of failure, since my fear of being left behind, being irrelevant, being less than good, I have been curtsying. I have been bowing in the name of work ethic. In the name of productivity. In the name of self-actualization and self-worth and happiness.

And I have decided to shift my eyes upward, to raise my head, to dust off my knees, and to walk swiftly in the opposite direction.

The blog post is my first tiptoe back into this journey. An excerpt:

We live in a world of more; this much is obvious. More things, more information. More time-saving tricks we use to find the time to uncover even more time-saving tricks. We live in a world of Pinterest, where visual images shoot out like firehoses of pretty, manifesting themselves in the parts of our brain we reserve for

planning elaborate feasts and fetes. We have hundreds of RSS subscriptions to blogs creating amazing tablescapes and Halloween costumes and DIY floor lamps. And we take it all in, bookmarking each project for future use when "someday" is finally today.

Yet . . . I fear that someday will never come. Because there will continually be more to do, to see, to buy. And our someday file will slowly become outdated with a new sea of ideas and thoughts promising to fulfill our lives in ways we never dreamed possible.

There is more noise, and my ears are tired.

I can no longer hear my own lion roar.

Within moments, the comments pour in. From Europe to Africa, from mothers to daughters, from art teachers to art students, my small corner of the internet breathes a sigh of relief.

And here I am, in my fleece-lined slippers, thinking I am the only one.

In a society that places a disproportionate emphasis on productivity, there is a true and real fear of slowing down. Will we be replaced? Left behind? Disrespected by the masses, whispered about in cubicles?

Will we be cast aside for not pulling our weight, for not keeping up with the pace, for not playing by the rules?

For exiting too slow on the 405?

Perhaps.

Perhaps we will be chastised, misunderstood. We might appear incompetent or lazy. We might be labeled meek.

Poor, lowly, plain.

But perhaps we will not.

Perhaps the meek *are* the blessed.

Perhaps cubicles are the true sanctuary, crouched down right there between the power cords and pencil cups. Not the corner office or the mahogany desk, not the pulpit or the stage. With or without the tie clip.

Not the front and center but the sidelines and the back rooms—the unseen, the unheard, the quiet hands that have already learned what the rest of us seek to know.

That there are blessings—peace, abundance, humility—in racing toward a different finish line.

That there is a difference between being left behind and placing others first.

That meek is not spiritless.

The following morning, while Bee naps and I reflect on yesterday's blog post, I am reminded of a passage from the Bible I memorized as a child. In Matthew 19:30, it is written, "But many who are first will be last, and many who are last will be first."

And I take my dusty Bible from the end table, and I turn the thin pages, and I underline the sentence and scrawl on a piece of junk mail a reminder: "Erin, keep slowing down. You've got a race to lose."

24.

WHEN YOU EDIT YOUR SOUL, NO ONE WINS

When you find out who you are, you will no longer be innocent. That will be sad for others to see. All that knowledge will show on your face and change it. But sad only for others, not for yourself. You will feel you have a kind of wisdom, very mistaken, but a mistake of some power to you and so you will sadly treasure it and grow it.
—*Lorrie Moore,* A Gate at the Stairs

If you choose to slow your life, to live intentionally, to subtract belongings or schedules or expectations—if you tell the truth about yourself to yourself—you will begin to notice tension around you.

Friends will gape, slack-jawed, in the vinyl restaurant booth when you tell them you've quit your job or are moving to another country, or no thanks on the creme brulee, you're taking a break from sugar. Sometimes they'll smile and ask questions, listen and nod, their foreheads wrinkling to make sense of it all. The best scenario is that you've all brought your kids to dinner and the baby begins to fuss, and this is when everyone gets to cut the awkward conversation short and blame the kids. *It's getting late, isn't it? Let me grab the check.*

If you're like me, you'll let a few reactions downplay your words. You'll offer an excuse. You don't wish to offend, so you'll diminish the cause and squelch every ounce of passion that birthed the idea in the first place.

No one wants to hear their choices aren't enough for someone else.

What did Franz Kafka call it? The editing of your own soul?

This is not authenticity. Authenticity is not the watering down of your message to help someone accept your words. Authenticity, I think, is simply trying to find the kindest way to tell the whole truth.

My season of slowing down coincided with a reevaluation of the foods I was eating. I was raised, like many kids in my generation, on canned beef stew and microwave popcorn, on Wendy's cheeseburgers and french silk ice cream. It wasn't until I had to do my own grocery shopping in college that I realized green beans come from the ground, and wait, they are meant to be crunchy? What is this so-called produce section, and where are all of the cans?

Years later, a simple elimination of dairy products (Bee had been a fussy, vomiting newborn, and my midwife suggested a potential milk allergy was the cause) had snowballed into a mass exodus from the pantry. I prioritized my health, recovering from a season of takeout and lackluster nutrition. I checked out library books on healthful eating; I switched from butter to ghee. I compared the prices of dates. I went vegan for a week, a glorious transition until it occurred to me that bacon, no matter how it is positioned on the plate, cannot qualify as vegan.

And somewhere along the way, through the veggie chopping, the farmer's market wandering, the food label reading, I understood just how poor my eating habits had been.

In a culture in which nearly every holiday, every celebration, every family function is marked with a four-course meal, a food reevaluation is bound to become obvious within your social circle. Instead of bringing chips and dip to the family reunion picnic, I opted for veggies and guac. When friends came over for dinner, I served zucchini noodles in lieu of pasta.

Once, I brought raw brownies for a four-year-old's tea party, and she spit them out into our makeshift Earl Grey. "Miss Erin," she said to me, "these are

RAW BROWNIE RECIPE

I swear to you, these will taste nothing like dog treats. I have perfected my technique. Also, four-year-olds know nothing of goodness.

*Ingredients**

1 cup pitted medjool dates

1/2 cup cocoa powder

1/3 cup almonds

Pinch of sea salt

001. Blend all ingredients with a spoon or mixer or whatever you've got. (The texture might be a bit sticky, so use some persistence here. I believe in you.)

002. Form your brownies in a glass airtight container. I like to make little balls with mine (they make for easy snacking!), but you can also press them down into a square pan or dish and cut them accordingly.

003. Try not to eat them in one day. But it happens, so go easy on yourself, okay?

This is a good base, but play around a bit. If you like sweet brownies, add a few more pitted dates. For more chocolate, spoon in some extra cocoa powder. I just eyeball my ingredients because it makes each batch taste slightly different than another, and who doesn't love some old-fashioned variety?

not called brownies. These are called dog treats."

With the change in my diet, I began to enjoy cooking. Creativity abounds when you're no longer limiting yourself to freezer sections and drive-thru lanes, and I remember this season as a rich time of growth in the kitchen.

Some friends remember this season as a rich time of my annoying waitresses from the vinyl booth: *I'm so sorry, but can you leave the seasoning off? Dressing on the side? Do you have any coconut milk in the kitchen, or even almond milk? Okay, none for me, thanks.*

A few friends reaped the benefits. I tested new recipes from library cookbooks and passed along the best of the best. We were tiny test kitchens in the form of group text messaging, and along the way, an impromptu cooking club was born. *Has anyone ever used coconut aminos? Worth the price?* (*Yes*, we said. *Yes, yes, yes!*)

There was one friend, though, who remained silent. I had assumed she was busy with her newborn—she had just given birth a few weeks prior; I had brought the non-dog-treat brownies—but it wasn't until weeks later that I knew the true reason for the crickets.

As we sit in our favorite coffee shop, as she spoons her triple fudge frappe and I sip a hot tea, she asks me how the whole cooking thing is going.

Worth noting, I think, is that if anyone adds "the whole" and "thing" to either side of your current passion, this is not a good sign.

"I just think you're idolizing food, that's all," she says. "You're taking it too seriously. A burger's not gonna kill you. Stop trying to be perfect."

I had wanted her support. I had wanted her acceptance. I had wanted her to applaud me, to inspire me, to encourage me to stay the course. I had wanted her to be a cheerleader for the change, to wave a spatula, to decorate an apron, to shout, "I'm right there with you, sister! Let's get healthy!"

I had at least wanted her kindness.

She did not offer it. And as months went by, each time she shifted her weight in a vinyl restaurant booth, I felt sympathetic to her discomfort, and I edited my own soul and ordered the burger.

And I resented her.

Do you want to know a secret? I was proud of myself. I had compromised my beliefs to foster a relationship. I had empowered my friend. I had allowed her to win.

But when you edit your soul, no one wins.

Do you want to know the harder thing, harder than the change itself? The harder thing is to know when you're ordering the burger for yourself, and when you're ordering the burger to make someone else feel better.

The harder thing is to notice when you're editing your soul, scissors in hand, and you've cropped an authentic friendship right out of the picture because you weren't strong enough to tell the truth.

I have edited my soul many times, and each time, I've done so in the name of kindness. Good intentions. Passivity.

I have quieted my gut, silenced my mind, tightened my lips. I have done this in marriage, in friendships, in life. Just yesterday, an acquaintance asked me for relationship advice while crying into her tea: "Should I leave him?"

And even though I wanted to shout from the mountaintops, "No! You can get through this one! I can feel it! I know the best therapist ever! Hold on!" I did not. I swallowed hard, and I passed her a tissue, and I told her she is the only one who can answer that.

And she is. She is the only one who can answer that.

But I was the only one who, in that moment, could offer support. I was the only one sitting in the kitchen, sipping my ginger tea, believing in her marriage and not telling her so.

I wasn't strong enough to offer any part of my soul, to give my honest advice. What if I was wrong? What if the marriage crumbled, if she resented me for my opinion, if he broke

THE HARDER THING IS TO NOTICE WHEN YOU'RE EDITING YOUR SOUL, SCISSORS IN HAND, AND YOU'VE CROPPED AN AUTHENTIC FRIENDSHIP RIGHT OUT OF THE PICTURE BECAUSE YOU WEREN'T STRONG ENOUGH TO TELL THE TRUTH.

her heart again, if the damage was irreparable and it was all my fault?

I was strong enough only to offer a tissue.

"You're going to be okay," I said.

Last spring I took a partner yoga class on an early morning in San Francisco. The morning clouds hadn't yet lifted and the group was chilled, foggy. Our instructor—a pixied brunette with at least eight visible piercings—stalked with a straight spine, straight legs, straight face to the front of the group and clapped her hands twice. Her voice was quiet, her tone loud. "Up and at 'em, guys. It's time to open those hearts. It's time to wake up the sun!"

We grouped into boy-girl pairs—strangers in leggings—and she taught us how to master assisted backbends, bound angle poses, something Twizzlerish called a reverse camel. And then she taught us flying bow and wheel pose, and then I understood something I hadn't understood before.

In flying bow and wheel pose, the "base" lies on his back with his hands and feet positioned upward, like he's balancing a heavy plank of wood. The other partner—the "flier"—leans her lower back into the base's feet, preparing for a back bend. As the base slowly straightens his legs to a vertical position, the flier leans back, releasing her shoulders into his outstretched hands.

The flier is in a floating backbend, and the base is supporting her weight. The base is not pulling her down. He is not changing his mind. He is waiting. He is remaining. He is quietly, patiently staying his course.

"Can you feel your hearts opening?" our instructor asks. "Can you feel the lightness? Can you see the sun?"

Here's the funny thing about this pose. It appears that the base is pushing back the flier, and in a sense, he is. He is creating an unchanging foundation that the flier can trust herself with, can allow herself to lean into. Only then can her heart be opened, softened, stretched.

It looks like he's pushing. It looks as if he will not budge.

One's tension enables another's ease.

One's strength allows another's softness.

One's firmness offers another's flexibility.

When we choose to be authentic in our relationships, when we choose to stand firm, we are offering a strong base. There is tension in this, but it is the precise amount of tension that another might need to soften, to flex, to change if they'd like.

As we fall out of the pose and switch positions, as the flier becomes the base and the base becomes the flier, I think of my friend. I think of the burgers, of the resentment.

I had not offered a strong base. I had not offered much of anything.

We think surrender means rolling over onto our backs. We think it means waving a white flag and compromising our beliefs to comfort another. We think surrender means ordering the burger.

Surrender does not mean ordering the burger.

To surrender is to be strong. It is to accept the tension for what it is. It is to notice the white flag, to acknowledge the burger, and to choose, instead, to say, both to yourself and to another, "This is what I am today. This is who I can offer. Take it, if you'd like."

Sometimes the one surrendering is not the flier, in the air, on her back.

Sometimes the one surrendering is the base. Strong, firm, supportive.

I return home from San Francisco to find that my friend's baby will be dedicated later that weekend at church. I mark it on the calendar and send her a text.

"Can I bring brownies?" I ask. "They're vegan."

"No way!" she writes.

"Your loss," I joke.

My friend did not turn vegan. She stayed authentic to her own self. After all, wisdom is little more than knowing what works for you and forgetting the rest.

We meet for coffee every now and then, and she sometimes gives me a side glance for ordering a hot tea when I used to go for a triple chocolate anything.

But it doesn't matter. Our hearts are open to different things.

What matters is, simply, that they are open to each other.

What matters is that we have surrendered the fight.

25.

IN PURSUIT OF OURSELVES

"We're all fools," said Clemens, "all the time. It's just we're a different
kind each day. We think, I'm not a fool today. I've learned my lesson.
I was a fool yesterday but not this morning. Then tomorrow
we find out that, yes, we were a fool today too. I think the
only way we can grow and get on in this world is to accept
the fact we're not perfect and live accordingly."
—*Ray Bradbury,* The Illustrated Man

I could surrender the fight with others. I could cast aside the comparison and resentment in friendships, the expectations and scorecards in marriage.

But could I cast these aside in myself?

There is a story in the Bible that I believe to be true, and it is a simple one, and a profound one, and one that changed the course of our souls, the plane of our landscape. It's one we've heard before, a million times over, and it still rings true every minute of my life.

It's the story of two humans trading the mounds of fresh fruit they'd been given for a single apple, bitten and bruised. It's the story of two hearts trading contentment for information. Trading what they had for what they wanted to have.

Trading everything for more.

And in pursuit of the better, Adam and Eve lost the good.

In pursuit of knowledge, they lost wisdom.

In pursuit of themselves, they lost themselves.

Do you know what happens after Adam and Eve make their trade, after they choose forbidden fruit for a lifetime of sin? As the story goes, they immediately cover themselves and hide from God.

"Then the eyes of both of them were opened, and they realized they were naked; so they sewed fig leaves together and made coverings for themselves" (Gen. 3:7).

What am I looking for?

Fastened on a canvas and propped on a shelf in my office is a pair of sequined gold shorts—a flattened, tailored disco ball of weird—to remind me of my own fig leaf moment a few years ago.

I was scheduled to give the keynote speech at a conference and was feeling wildly insecure. It was January. There were mountains of leftover holiday cheese raging through my insides, and the weather was unusually and aggressively cold, the kind of cold that leaves your knuckles splitting in revolt. I felt dark and bumpy and naked, and the conference was two weeks away, and I was unbelievably seasonally brain-dead.

I was also eight weeks pregnant with Bee, and pregnancy brain, I'd discovered, is what happens when you give your normal-person brain space to a fetus and they promptly suck you dry of all reasoning skills, slurpy alien style.

And so here I was—pregnant with a kidney bean who was stealing any mildly coherent thoughts—having written zero words of the speech I was scheduled to give, and I decided this would be a perfectly reasonable moment to shop online.

It was *not* a perfectly reasonable moment to shop online, as I'm sure you have gathered, and I left for that conference with a suitcase of new clothing—sequined shorts notwithstanding—and not a word written for my keynote.

It was, as you'd imagine, a disaster. A sideshow spectacle, really, in which the girl in the sequined shorts and mock turtleneck—Aspen chic, I called that ensemble—broke out in a cold sweat and had to sit down on the floor in the middle of her presentation and announce to the live telecast that I'm so sorry; I'm newly pregnant and the baby has stolen all of my thoughts and I'm having trouble catching my breath, but look how cute these shorts are?

My sequined fig leaves—like Adam and Eve's—did not serve me well, although they did get a good laugh.

What would have happened if I'd paused and truly felt that expanse? If I'd allowed the inadequacy, perhaps offered myself rest? What if I'd taken deep breaths or slowed my runaway-freight-train thoughts long enough to think logically and realistically? What if I'd bravely arrived—eyes to eyes, nose to nose—at the very thought I feared: that I was deeply and utterly inadequate?

I believe that had I stopped searching for a fig leaf, I would have instead found an olive branch. I believe I would have discovered the peace that comes only after you throw up your hands, throw in the towel, and say, "God? Please help the sister in the sequined shorts."

The unborn baby who stole my brilliant mind is growing up now, and the most brilliant parenting advice I've received boils down to some version of this:

I BELIEVE THAT HAD I STOPPED SEARCHING FOR A FIG LEAF, I WOULD HAVE INSTEAD FOUND AN OLIVE BRANCH.

Let her fail. Let her feel bored and restless and inadequate. Hold her hand when she feels intimidated or fearful or small. Look into her cerulean eyes and say, "I am here. I understand. I cannot take this away, but I will walk next to you, right here. I will be right here."

I have to fight the urge—daily—to cover her with fig leaves. I have to force myself to avoid parenting in a sterile white bathroom with a medicine cabinet stocked with my own bandaids: distracting gadgets, misplaced blame, painted smiles.

The sequined shorts, quietly displayed on their high shelf, remind me that this is a choice. That I can choose the world's fig leaves to cover my stretch marks, dark circles, battle scars.

Or I can choose to accept my lessness and reach for more: more grace, more gentleness, more peace. I can surrender the fig leaves. I can lay down the cloak. I can remove the mask. And I can choose to look above, naked and trembling, searching the denim sky for an olive branch to grasp and carry and keep.

Do you want to know the best way to accept your flaws? It is to practice accepting someone else's.

His name is Cam. He comes into the coffee shop where I write each day, and he is—how shall I put this?—strenuous.

Cam is legally blind, and he strides—I cannot find the word for his stride, because it is something of a clump, really—into the coffee shop in his long braids and navy bandana and drops next to me, begins his barrage of questions. Each morning, it is the same.

Cam: "Whatcha your name, lady?"

Erin: . . .

Cam: "Karen?"

Erin: "Cam, you know me! We do this every morning."

Cam: "Ha, yeah, yeah, yeah, yeah, we do. Hey. Wouldya look somethin' up for me?"

Erin: "The Yankees ranking?" [Also insert Amazon's customer service phone number or anything Hillary Clinton.]

Cam: "Man, how'd you know? You're clairvescent, aren't ya?"

Erin: "Clairvoyant?"

Cam: "Same."

When I'm in the middle of a paragraph and anxious to get home to Bee, Cam's infinite questions are taxing. He's charming . . . and annoying. But I am learning to smile when he interrupts my thought to tell me the knock-knock joke about the banana

("Orange you glad?") for the third time this week. I am learning to set my homepage to ESPN for the latest baseball news.

Spiritual teacher Ram Dass once wrote that we should treat everyone we meet like they are God in drag, and so I try. It is difficult. God is very persistently losing the phone number to Amazon's customer service to return the Nikes he bought the week prior.

And yet there is grace. It abounds for me and it abounds for Cam, and it's just that . . . I don't know . . . use it or lose it.

Once I begin using it—on me and on others—I stop counting my transgressions at night. It's easier to sleep when Cam has exhausted you, when you're emptied of your grace and in the morning another dose waits for you both, like the sun.

I used to confuse the words *grace* and *goodwill.*

I would read the front page of CNN.com and wonder how grace abounds for the killers, the gunmen, the liars, the thieves. These people do not warrant goodwill. Their actions are not justifiable. When judged, their sins far outweigh their good behavior, tip the scale far in the direction of undeserving.

So I'd try to give them a free pass. I'd try to envision their lives as difficult, as broken. I'd remind myself that hurt people hurt people, that we're all in this together, doing our best, fighting hard battles, winning some and losing most. And I'd wish them goodwill. I'd offer them what I thought was grace.

Hurt people do hurt people.

We're all fighting hard battles.

These are worthy perspectives.

This is not grace.

Grace is not giving someone else a free pass because they've had a hard day. Grace is not giving yourself a free pass because you've had a hard day. Grace is not explaining away our bad behavior, then shrugging our shoulders and saying, "Hey, what're you gonna do? It is what it is. Who wants ice cream?"

Sure, I want the free pass. But this is me justifying an action—someone else's or my own—by offering goodwill. This is me searching for an explanation that I can understand instead of accepting the one I will never be able to understand.

That we have already been forgiven.

That we have already been set free.

Still, I offer my version of grace:

You did this wrong, but look, you did that right. Don't beat yourself up. Here, have a fig leaf. Would you like some tea? Can I get you anything?

God's version of grace is this:

You did this wrong, but look, I did this right. You have everything you need now. Follow me in peace. Go now in freedom.

Walk now in abundance.

Grace is giving yourself a free pass and realizing that it isn't free at all.

Grace is giving someone else a free pass and realizing God has already passed his along.

To all of us.

I talked with Cam a few weeks ago. He asked who I'd be voting for in the next election, told me to google Hillary Clinton again, told me not to worry, he didn't order the Nikes. (He did order the Nikes.) And then he told me something else.

"Woman, did ya know I'm schizophrenic?" he said.

I asked him if he was being serious, and I asked him not to call me woman.

"Ah, I'm sorry, Karen," he said. "But yeah, for real!"

And he told me that's why he couldn't get grace. He'd done too many things wrong, that the bad guys in him keep screwing with the good guys in him. "And woman," he says, "the bad dudes just keep on winnin'."

I don't think he's talking about grace. I think he's talking about goodwill.

I often hear women, in the church aisle or at the coffee shop or in passing at the grocery store, beating themselves up. We're good at this. We're great at swimming in guilt, gifted at wading the waters of our own regret, mistakes, missteps.

When we're not covering ourselves with fig leaves to mask our sins, we're covering ourselves with guilt to bear our punishment. We've been found guilty of spending too much time on our phones, of spending too much money at Target, of spending too little time on meal planning. We say the wrong things at the right time, or the right things

GRACE IS GIVING YOURSELF A FREE PASS AND REALIZING THAT IT ISN'T FREE AT ALL.

at the wrong time. We're too much and we're too little and we wonder if we'll ever be enough. If we'll ever deserve favor.

We've been tried, and we are guilty of it all.

Surely we don't deserve goodwill?

But goodwill is not what we have been promised.

What we have been promised is grace.

Amazing grace! How sweet the sound
That saved a wretch like me!
I once was lost, but now am found;
Was blind, but now I see.

Cam is still blind. He's still schizophrenic. He's still beating himself up on some days, still ordering Nikes on others, still asking about Hillary and the Yankees nearly every morning. But these are questions I can figure out. These are questions with answers I can find. And answering them with patience is a small bit of goodwill I can afford.

And so, every morning, I am learning to offer goodwill. (Mostly.)

And every morning, God offers grace.

To both of us.

Amazing.

00

26.

THE GAME OF GIVE

See, I am doing a new thing! Now it springs up; do you not perceive it?
I am making a way in the wilderness and streams in the wasteland.
—Isaiah 43:19

"Y ou just have to die to yourself," my friend says.

We are waltzing around her farmhouse table cleaning up the remnants of a successful afternoon snack for her three kids: dried hummus smeared on the tabletop, rice-cracker crumbs nestled in the cracks of the wood beams. She is scrubbing an ominous dollop of tomato sauce on her son's place-mat, and she smiles. "I cannot remember the last time I made pasta. Where did this even come from?"

Bee is on my hip, and I laugh know-ingly, but not at all knowingly. I am new to this. We are only eight months into mother-and-daughter, into pasta-maker and pasta-spiller. There is no homework to tackle, no anatomy conversations to navigate, no bullies to confront. It is simple.

It is not easy.

I adjust Bee on my hip—we are not yet entirely comfortable together—and I ask how my friend manages three kids, a home, a social calendar, a life. We women are prone to calling this the juggle, the great balancing act of motherhood, but really, I just want to know how she can keep up with the laundry.

"It gets easier," she says, emptying clean forks from the dishwasher as Bee begins to fuss in my arms. It's time for another diaper change and I'm down to the last diaper, and I realize that as much as I want to stay here around the farmhouse table, as much as I want to ask my friend for more advice, more tips, more secrets, I know neither of us has the answers.

Motherhood is sometimes just a matter of going to the grocery for more diapers when you really want another spoonful of Nutella and some good old-fashioned neighborly gossip.

I know of this quest for more. Women who want it all, who strive to excel in everything, who need to perfect each and every category. We want to wake up with sexy tousled hair, kiss our husband on the lips, walk to an early morning barre class while the baby bounces quietly in our organic carrier, meet our girlfriends for a cold-pressed juice before changing into our power suit and heel-toeing it to the seventeenth-floor office as our eldest, a sophomore—*What? You have a soph-omore? You look amazing!*—earns early entry into Yale and arrives home from his swim meet in time to compliment the free-range egg quiche we just whipped up with herbs from the backyard garden.

This cannot be the ideal. This cannot be the standard.

I leave my girlfriend's house and strap Bee into her car seat, already anticipating the tantrum to come. It is late, and we need diapers, and I have forgotten to bring Puffs to distract her from the general contempt she feels at this hour. The crying begins.

I drive to the grocery store quickly, and I park, and Bee's tears have not subsided. I am now the frazzled mother in yoga pants you see at your local Kroger, comparing prices of deli meat while fishing a blueberry out of the baby's ear.

Give me diapers or give me death, I think, and I whisper mantras to myself as I cross the parking lot. This does no good for the mental portrait I am painting: frazzled mother in yoga pants is now talking to herself. Get in and get out. You can do this. This will pass. The crying will end.

Inside, Bee is inconsolable. The

harsh lights and stark air-conditioning of the grocery anger her, and she contorts her face, exclaiming her discontent as I rush through the diaper aisle.

My friend is right. You do have to die to yourself, in a way. You have to die of embarrassment, you have to die to your need for control, your desire to hide away your insecurities with a fresh cut and color at the salon.

I don't want to have it all. But I realize, here in the grocery store checkout line, that I do want to have what I used to have: control, freedom, predictability, confidence, time, energy, flexibility.

Which parts of me must break down to create more space for another?

Do you know how a coral reef is created? It's formed by its own breakdowns. It cracks from the wind, the water, the elements, and then something new and vibrant is created in its place. Its very shape changes, like a mother—rounding, forming, growing altogether lovely.

The break itself is the beauty.

The crack is worthy of gold.

I pay for the diapers. We find the car as the sun turns peach, and I strap Bee into the car seat harness, feeling rattled and defeated by our misadventure at the grocery.

As I start the car and glance into the rearview mirror, I am startled by our reflection. There are two of us.

Two of us.

Once there was just one. Once it was just me, and now it is more than just me. It is me and Bee. Me and a baby. Me and my daughter.

It is startling when your brain catches up with reality, when your mind finally wraps its thread around your thumb enough to make a loop, to come to a realization, to a full understanding of what truly is.

Bee is quiet in her car seat behind me, lashes heavy as rest finally finds her. I peek at her in the rearview mirror, and I know that she knows only grunts and sounds, Dada and Moo, and I have read that she can already sense danger, that she can already feel love, that she can already comprehend the wide range of human emotion.

And here I am, in the front, struggling to make room for it all. Here I am, peeking at my reflection in the mirror, expecting to see one, expecting to see me, but instead seeing two.

There is a mother and a daughter with tired eyes fighting the wind, the water, the elements. I must make room.

ANDES MTNS

No more than two years later, on the base of the Andes mountains, hiking in cold boots behind the wind-whipped hair of my friend Mara and her husband, Danny, I experience my own breakdown, my coral reef moment, my own kintsugi. I learn what it means to truly love every piece of myself.

With every piece of myself.

Mara and Danny were teaching classes on an organic farm in South America and asked if we'd like to bring Bee along, to take a class, to experience change.

"We have llamas!" she'd emailed.

You never say no to a llama.

During the trip, we hiked and we listened and we learned. We fed horses and fish, we bought coffee at the markets, we watched documentaries on change, on nutrition, on meditation.

And then the conversation that changed it all.

"I had been basing my value on circumstances I couldn't control," Mara says during the hike. "I had been basing my value on motherhood, on my job, on my status as a good wife. And when I failed in those areas, my worth took the hit."

Have I been doing the same?

Have I been basing my value on my job?

"A bad day at the office could render me useless, horizontal on the sofa, eating blue fish gummies and mourning my lack of luck."

On my motherhood?

"I am chasing a new identity—that of a working mother who has achieved a perfect balance."

On my status as a good wife?

"And this is where I am, in the kitchen with the note and the peonies, sweating in my sweater, resentment oozing from my pores."

Have I become weighted by circumstances I can't control? By the brain tumor, the bankruptcy, by the bad days and the good?

We were meant to keep an eye on it.

But if we aren't keeping an eye on things, how will we know their value? If there is nothing to tally, how will we know their worth?

How will we know our own?

My mind is spinning, from the high altitude and the sore calves and the cold hiking boots, and I hear Mara say one last thing before I crouch on the side of the mountain to offer myself a breath.

"You get to decide," she says. "It's a choice. You get to decide to place your worth somewhere else. In something else. In something beyond circumstances."

In something beyond yourself.

The thing about love is that time shifts it into new shapes, like water on a rock. The thing about love is that everything else is sand.

Try again, this time with less you and more water.

When I think of love, I think of compatibility and sacrifice, of commitment and service. Of give-and-take. But only part of this is true.

Love is not a game of take.

Love is only a game of give.

I get this wrong daily, I think. I make small relational kinks into big issues, ironing out my discomforts in the name of love. In the name of math. I keep score. I expect my love to be returned to the same degree in which it is given. *I gave you a birthday present; you didn't even call.* I create expectations to smooth the waters, to navigate my course, to keep the ship under control.

And yet, sometimes, choppy waters teach us to sail better.

Bee is a toddler now, and yesterday she had a slew of tantrums at home. She wanted to play with her sand outside, but it was raining, and her gloom permeated our home like the smell of burnt popcorn—one whiff was enough to send the whole house into despair. No, she did not want a snack. No, she did not want to dance. No, she did not want to go to the library. *No, no, no!*

On a normal day, before I learned what it means to love without expectation, a bad day for Bee meant a bad day for me. Surely her tantrums defined me; surely they were a reflection of how ill-suited I am to parent her. Certainly this is our future snowballing before us: daughter acting unkind, mother reacting unkindly, two polarizing fields building until the bond between them is broken, pushed to opposite ends of the room—or country.

But I learned something about love, and identity, when walking with my friends in the Andes mountains. I learned that when we define our worth by circumstances, even the valid ones—I am a wife, I am a mother, I am a writer—our worth will always be in question. And when our worth is in question, we react to our failures with fear or despair or anger.

If I am defined by my writing, what happens when I feel creatively blocked?

If I am defined by my mothering, what happens when Bee has a tantrum in Target?

If I am defined by my marriage, what happens when Ken and I are fighting over who lost the keys and made us late to our nephew's baptism, and *Good gracious, no, that is not the kind of thing you can be late to—what kind of godparent are you?*

When we strip away every circumstantial identity—writer, mother, wife—we are left with the only identity that can never be in question: I am a woman of God.

Therefore, *I am a woman of Love.*

When we define ourselves as women and men of God or of Love or of Light or of whatever name forces us out of the small role we are playing into the gloriously intricate story woven into this world, our worth is no longer in question.

We are loved.

We are loved by God.

We are love.

Nothing can threaten this truth. No ill-timed reaction or toddler tantrum can take it away. We are secure. Our worth is safe.

Yesterday, as the rain poured down outside and Bee's tears flowed inside, we sat in the sunroom and watched the storm.

"I'm sorry I yelled," I said. "I love you even when you're whining. Do you know that?"

"Yeah," she said, engrossed in a puzzle. "Can I have a smoothie?"

And as the rain beat down onto the deck, as the puddles spilled onto the grass below, as the drops made mosaics of the window, I went to the kitchen to make a smoothie. I offered her love.

The smoothie was easy.

The love was hard.

We both drank in abundance.

THE "LOVE YOUR KID UNCONDITIONALLY" SMOOTHIE

Ingredients

1 cup chocolate almond milk or chocolate
  coconut water

1 small frozen banana

1 cup frozen raspberries

1 Tbsp cocoa powder

1 Tbsp chia seeds

Optional: a few fresh mint leaves to balance
  the sweetness, and for garnish

*You know what to do by now, right? Good.
Happy blending!*

27.

I BLAME THE GLITTER

For just one second, look at your life and see how perfect it is.
Stop looking for the next secret door that is going to lead you to
your real life. Stop waiting. This is it: there's nothing else. It's here,
and you'd better decide to enjoy it or you're going to be miserable
wherever you go, for the rest of your life, forever.
—*Lev Grossman,* The Magicians

Sometimes I feel whole. And sometimes I feel like a fraud, like my life is cropped out of the square images of my Instagram feed. I crop, you crop, we all crop for comments.

Today I am interviewed by *New York Magazine* for an article on blog "celebrities" and the toll that sort of success takes on one's personal life. The reporter's assistant sends an email asking me to offer my perspective on the internet, authenticity, and criticism online: What is it like having your life publicly scrutinized? Is negativity the price you pay for broadcasting your life to the masses? Is criticism justified when it arrives in emoji grids and anonymous comments? Is anyone and everyone entitled to shout their opinions into the megaphone of social media?

I do not know the answers to her

questions, but the phone rings, and I answer. The reporter and I swap motherhood stories and I warm to her immediately as we chat about recent travels, summer plans, and then a question.

"Is your house really that white and perfect?"

I am caught off guard. I have taken the phone interview in my bedroom, where I am sitting crosslegged on my unmade bed. To my right, the twisted plug of our carpet cleaner—the dog has peed again—peeks out from under a pile of laundry in need of folding, sorting, storing. To my left, the open window reveals a back yard overtaken by weeds and the rotting remains of a hand-me-down wooden swingset badly in need of repair.

Just this morning, I discovered a blue chalk doodle on the wall in front of me, evidence of Bee's creative but maddening habit of drawing "murals" in every room of the home. (We're working on it.)

I do not remember how I answer the question. I remember only that in answering the question, I begin to question it all.

Am I encouraging perfection within my own white walls? Am I promoting consumerism each time I share the newest mascara,

I DO NOT REMEMBER HOW I ANSWER THE QUESTION. I REMEMBER ONLY THAT IN ANSWERING THE QUESTION, I BEGIN TO QUESTION IT ALL.

the floral notebook, the graphic "But First, Coffee" tee? Am I offering the false impression that this eco-friendly wooden toy will make you a better mother? That this brambleberry lip stain will make you a better wife? That the new Eckhart Tolle book, the new Birkenstocks, the new fill-in-the-blank will make you a better woman?

Have I created a standard? Have I been doling out small, stale consumerist bread crumbs when what readers need—what we all need—is a tall drink of water?

I am no longer listening, and the interview is finished. The reporter says goodbye, and I lean back on my duvet. The dogs stir. I am recalling the phone conversation, the reporter's questions, her curiosity about the state of my perfect little white home.

And I will tell you this: my house is not perfect.

And I will tell you this: my house is perfect.

Yours is too.

It is both and it is neither. It matters only what we see.

I have been keeping an eye on this.

In Los Angeles, on Catalina Avenue, I saw rusty porch swings. I saw the dirty bar down on the corner, the chain-link fence down the street, the ocean just blocks away, but would you look at that garbage can overflowing onto the pier? Ugh.

In the Midwest, on Bent Hollow, I saw a dying father-in-law in a hospice bed. I saw childhood sheets. I saw bankruptcy, failure, midnight crossword puzzles, and the occasional cheerful houseplant.

And now, on Winterfield, in this gloriously imperfectly perfect home, I see everything. I see how blue chalk marks on white walls can make you smile one day and drive you mad the next. I see that this is okay. I see that this is good.

I see that this is not perfect.

And I see that it is perfect, that everything is as it should be, that all is accounted for, that the imperfection lies only in my perspective.

I see that a messy pantry is cause not for a reorganizational purge but a prayer of gratitude for plenty. Nourishment.

I see that a sink full of dirty dishes presents not a mindless chore but lingering evidence of a gift. Community.

I see that overturned glitter in a toddler's bedroom is not a personal affront, an intentional interruption in my day, but a child's attempt to capture beauty. Creativity.

And I see that when I miss the mark, when I fail to see these gifts as gifts and see them as a long list of daily defeats, this is okay too.

A speck of dust in my eye, that's all. (I blame the glitter.)

It takes work to change your perspective, work that is not easily done when you're looking everywhere else.

Once when I was a kid, my grandparents took me to a mall with a merry-go-round in the center. My sisters and cousins, fueled by sugary ice cream, piled onto circus animals—decorated elephants, costumed horses, clown cars. The music began; the carousel blurred.

I grew sick after the first orbit as I watched the crowds, the masses, the faces all become a cloud of oblivion. I dizzied, and I rested my head on the jeweled camel to my side.

My cousin Maria shouted over the pouncing tiger she'd saddled, "Just focus on one point! Look at the center!"

This is hard to do today. It is hard to focus on one point when there are a million faces in your crowd. There are hundreds of friends, acquaintances, colleagues on your Instagram feed sharing their own bejeweled camels, their own painted donkeys. The big tent looks brighter from the outside. And have you seen that three-ring circus cake on Pinterest?

It is enough to make you lose your focus. It is enough to dizzy us all.

It's a fear of missing out on things, perhaps. What if we're going through life—in the carpool lane, at the grocery, on a conference call—with what we think is our signature lip shade of Brambleberry Stain when, in fact, all along we're meant to be a Rose 04-L?

What if the reason no one else seems to have gigantic suitcases under their eyes is because they've all discovered the magical tightening serum on clearance while we've been distracted by the cucumber exfoliant?

On paper, and on a good day, I know these doubts to be silly and trivial and enormously vain. But in my head, on a bad day, with wet hair and an empty coffee cup, when my toddler is playing bongo drums on my rear and I can feel the jiggle-jiggle, the silly and trivial and enormously vain seeps in and I jot down a mental note to peruse Amazon reviews for Spanx.

You simply cannot imagine the frustration this causes my husband, Ken. He will do the good and worthy work of offering me a compliment on my latest skin regimen—*Yes, your chin does seem to be clearing up!*—and then, two weeks later, I've switched up the routine and there is a Mount St. Helens right there on my nose.

"Why mess up a good thing?" he asks.

"Because I wanted to try out a better thing," I reply.

My house is not perfect. Your house is not perfect.

Our lives aren't, either.

And yet they're as they should be. They are uniquely ours, dizzy with the choices that have shaped our past, that are shaping our now. We are doing ourselves no favors when we look to the crowd to tell us where we are.

We are here. We are riding our painted horses into the sunset, our jeweled camels through the desert. We are here, today, for now, and you can simply forget about the rest.

Buy the brambleberry lip stain if you like.

It won't make you happier, but you needn't beat yourself up when it doesn't.

Perhaps this just means that your color isn't brambleberry but is white, with an errant blue chalk doodle mixed in for good measure.

WE ARE DOING OURSELVES NO FAVORS WHEN WE LOOK TO THE CROWD TO TELL US WHERE WE ARE.

28.

CALL IT BEAUTY

Do not spoil what you have by desiring what you have not; remember that
what you now have was once among the things you only hoped for.
—*Epicurus*

It is Saturday afternoon. We are hosting an out-of-town friend and I have chosen this as a perfectly acceptable time to transform Bee's nursery into a "big girl" room with her own toddler bed. After an enormous brunch of eggs and bacon, potatoes and avocados, coffee and berries, as the spring sun begins its late rise into the day, my pulse signals that it's time for a bit of productivity. *Enough with the rest, Loechner*, it says. *You've got a deadline to meet.*

The nursery project has been sponsored, which in the blogging world means you are being paid to accept product from a favorite company you'd likely have purchased from anyway, and you simply have to photograph said product in your home and tell your readers where you found it.

It's more complicated than that, of course, and I am oversimplifying. There are deadlines and endless marketing meetings, photo shoots and preproduction lists, and there is nearly always a list of marketing language the brand requires. I was once told to describe a water pitcher as an "overflowing fountain of youth," and, well, I suppose that's when I decided to throw in the towel with that particular brand.

But it's what we do. It is our job, a pungent soup of truth and beauty, of airbrush and edits. And there is a lot to be said for what has been edited out.

As Ken and our guest clean the dishes and wipe down countertops, I unpack the cardboard mountain in the corner of the dining room. There is an entire room to assemble: a dresser, a toddler bed, two bookcases, a dollhouse, piles of bedding and curtains, pillows and toys.

There is an overwhelming amount, and it occurs to me that I am less than grateful.

I am splicing open the cardboard boxes, thinking only of my deadline. Bee is playing in a sea of packing peanuts, jumping excitedly for her *Very own bed!* and her *Very own pillow!* and her *Very own dresser!* and I am here in the corner searching for the screwdriver. "Not yet, honey," I say. "We have a lot of work to do."

When did I become ungrateful? How did it come to this?

I am well aware of the perks of my job. I receive free clothing, free furniture, free trips—and of course, we all know by now that little is free. Everything arrives with the high cost of expectation, with the price of anticipated promotion.

And yet boxes pile up at our front door daily, and it seems our home has become one more stop on the consumerist railroad. I am forever dropping off the excess at the thrift store or offering close friends new wardrobe staples and beauty products. Mostly, it's fun. Just yesterday, a calf-hair backpack from Israel showed up moments after a girlfriend was asking if I had a spare bag she could borrow for her upcoming trek to the Middle East.

See? Fun.

Other times, I have difficulty seeing past the mess, the piles, the more. It feels a bit like shoveling snow in a blizzard, a constant cycle of purging just before the mailman arrives with a new binge.

And this is where I am on an otherwise beautiful spring Saturday afternoon. I see the binge, and I want the purge.

As the packing peanuts spread into the living room and the mess multiplies into tiny plastic bags of nuts and bolts and miniature wrenches, Ken's mom calls. "It's a beautiful day. Can we take the canoe out on the pond to catch turtles?"

I give Ken a look that is not quite a no

and not quite a yes, but is more like *I am covered in packing tape. What do you think?* and Ken, wisely, offers to take Bee and our guest to Grandma's for some springtime fishing while I make headway on the room makeover.

Something spectacular happens with the turn of a season. It's a mile marker for the year, a tiny roadside sign that proposes a measurement for your days. With the first hint of spring, when the first tulip sprouts, you remember where you were last spring, and the one before that, and *Isn't that the late spring when Bill passed away? When we were living on Bent Hollow? Was it that long ago?*

The house is quiet now; my family has been gone for hours. I am picturing Bee on the pond, a canoe filled with the people she loves, sweaty tendrils framing her face, joy in her starry eyes, shrieks of glee as she works to catch her first turtle of the year, and I am not there. I am here, in a sea of stuff, moving assembled furniture around to create a big-girl room that might inspire the masses.

Is anything more inspiring than a toddler's starry eyes?

As I tighten the bolts on Bee's new floor mirror, I catch my reflection. I see sweat gathering at my hairline. I see discontent in my face. The sun is going down, the room

is almost finished. Tomorrow we will begin photographing the space and then it will be over. Then I'll have time for turtles.

As I pad into the kitchen for tea, I pass the cardboard boxes, the packing peanuts, the tiny nuts and bolts scattered like pennies on a fountain floor. I feel a twinge of guilt over a wasted day, and then I feel another twinge of guilt because of my lack of gratitude. How many mothers would love a room makeover for their little girls? How many women would be thrilled to offer their kids the gifts that show up unannounced on my doorstep six days of the week?

I boil the water as everyone arrives through the front door in a burst of elation—Ken, our guest, Bee, my mother-in-law—all sweaty from a day spent adventuring, still chattering about the fish they encountered, still talking over one another in excitement, and something inside of me shifts.

I am pursuing minimalism. I know this to be true. I want less, and I want simplicity, and I want to spend my days connecting and caring, not consuming and completing.

But.

More important than pursuing minimalism, for me, is pursuing gratitude. And I missed the mark today not because I was surrounded by stuff, assembling floor lamps and reorganizing toddler leggings into dresser drawers. I missed the mark not because I failed to be minimal. I missed the mark because I failed to be grateful.

Theologian Richard Foster once spoke of this in his book *Celebration of Discipline.* "The Disciplines are for the purpose of realizing a greater good," he writes. "In and of themselves they are of no value whatever. They have value only as a means of setting us before God so that he can give us the liberation we seek. The liberation is the end; the Disciplines are merely the means. They are not the answer; they only lead us to the Answer."

"Do you guys want some tea?" I ask, reaching into the pantry.

They do, and so we spend the next few moments sipping chamomile and recounting our hours spent, theirs on the water, mine on the shore.

I peer from the kitchen into the dining room to see the cardboard boxes still stacked high and spilling out into the living room, the hallway, the entryway. Bee is building a playhouse.

I walk over to the mess. "Hey, lady! Want to see your new room?" I ask Bee.

"Nope," she says, nestling into an over-sized box. "I like this one."

As I am writing this, a book called *The Life-Changing Magic of Tidying Up* is being passed from the purses to the diaper bags to the backpacks of my inner circle. It references the beauty, the independence, the creativity that bloom from a tidy, minimal life. It speaks of the joy you receive when you free yourself from your things, when you view how much the things you own own you and then, quick, bandaid ripping style, do something about it.

The book explains how to detach your-self from stuff and leaves you very much wanting to hop a flight to Thailand and stop wearing deodorant. After you read one chapter, you will throw out a box of old pasta from your pantry. After you read two chapters, you will throw out the sauce too.

But after you read three chapters of this book, something takes root inside of you. You suddenly throw out the crock pot, the hot pads, the colander (who needs a colander?), and your husband returns from a business trip to find you cutting leftover chicken with fabric scissors because you have given away your steak knife set.

THINGS BEE HAS "COLLECTED" FROM THE TRASH PILE IN THE PAST THREE DAYS

001. 4 rubber bands
002. 2 used toothpicks
003. 1 pile of leaves
004. 3 grocery flyers
005. 2 dried tea bags
006. 1 take-out coffee lid
007. 1 cotton ball

Obviously, I loved the book. It was written for me, about me, to me, and yet I live with two other very endearing humans who have a penchant for collections. I call my family sentimental, but in truth, they are borderline magpies. Bee collects rocks, beads, anything tiny that will stab your foot if walked upon, and she collects containers for her collections. Her room is not a place to sleep; it is a museum of prized possessions, an archaeological dig of unearthed treasures. Just yesterday, I found a pile of leaves in her dresser drawer.

"They are my nature socks," she says.

Ken's collections—CDs, cables, tools, indoor slippers (?)—are more organized and far less random, but they do need dusting, sorting, caretaking. They require time and space and more maintenance than I like to offer.

And yet these crazies are my family. I love them and their swirly mix of annoyances, just as they love me and my compulsion to rid our home of steak knives. The trick, it seems, is to let it be, let it be, let it be à la Mr. McCartney.

Slowing and subtracting—these are good and worthy things. And yet when they become the end and not the means? It is likely you will end up on the kitchen floor with your head in your hands, and you will cry over the inescapable clutter, and your toddler will bring you her nature socks.

"Feel better, Mama?"

You might not. You might not feel better, but you will say yes, and you will smile, and you will thank her for her thoughtfulness as you wipe the tears from your eyes and rise up to thaw the chicken for dinner.

And so if you visit my home, you will find your typical excess. It is not the home of a minimalist. It is, instead, the home of a minimalist who is waving her white flag on a boat to Thailand while her husband and toddler load sea glass down the hatch.

Years ago, I helped a friend in San Francisco decorate her new apartment. It had tall ceilings, gorgeous crown molding, a Victorian claw-foot tub in a white subway tile bathroom. There was natural light, an immaculate view of a small dog park and, just beyond, the whole of the city.

I was in town for a conference and it was the first of the month, so we hit the Alameda market on a cold June morning with hot Starbucks in hand and a long list of necessities in our minds: a midcentury headboard for the bedroom, an unframed vintage typography poster, an overdyed Indian rug, preferably pink tinged and faded with age. We passed by each aisle lined with discarded disco balls and brass etageres, we tried on decade-old feather hats, we sifted through hundreds of vintage Girl Scout badges and ephemera.

We didn't find anything on our list, but my friend did fall deeply in love with an antique wire-framed chandelier that hid tiny metal butterflies in every shade imaginable. "It reminds me of my dad," she told me as she peered closely at the chipped paint of the monarch, the wide wings of the blue morpho. "He used to collect butterflies. He told me once that a caterpillar gets to choose who he is, that he can call himself a caterpillar like the rest of them, or he can say he's going to be a butterfly someday. It's the caterpillar's choice."

"Buy it," I said.

"But does it match?" she asked.

If you love it, it matches. If you love it, for whatever reason, it works. If the vintage Corn Flakes poster makes you think of your grandfather's favorite late-night snack, hang it in your Victorian living room. Call it a study in contrast. Call it visual interest.

Call it beauty.

My friend and I spent the rest of the weekend ordering a headboard, a rug, the art we never found at Alameda. It arrived in spurts that month, and in thirty days, her apartment was decorated perfectly.

It has been six years since that weekend. My friend has lived through a slew of transitions, changing careers and moving to Portland, falling in love, then relocating to upstate New York with her husband to buy a tiny home with tall trees at the end of a winding road.

She recently showed me a photo of the kitchen they were remodeling together, and as she flipped through her phone's camera roll, I saw the butterflies.

"You kept the chandelier?" I asked.

"It's, like, the only thing I kept," she said. After marrying, the couple pared down their belongings before they left the city. They hosted stoop sales for their decor, listed sofas and end tables on Craigslist, donated boxes of books to the library. Old clothing went to the thrift store, cooking equipment they no longer used was offered to a mission.

And then there were the butterflies.

"You should've seen me," she said. "I couldn't bear to pack it and send it with the movers, so I brought it on the plane with me as my carry-on. Just Paul and me, that giant wire-framed chandelier on my lap like a prized baby."

Decorating with meaning takes time. It takes purpose and patience, and if you're lucky, once every six years or so, you'll find something you'll love enough to carry on a plane with you as you start your new life.

But there's a thirst to do it all at once. There's an instinct for completion, for filling your space, for padding your nest in the name of comfort and style so you can host the housewarming party and clink the glassware and say to the world, *Look!*

We're settled! Here we are! Let the fun begin! (But please, use coasters. No rings on the new coffee table.)

When we decorate from this place, we're creating a showroom. It's easy to do, to create a stunning home void of meaning, a stylish space that holds little comfort.

Even the most beautiful home can lack beauty.

But sometimes, in decorating and in life, if you wait long enough, you'll find it. You'll find the diamond in the rough, the treasure in the trash, the caterpillar hidden deep within the cocoon.

The one you'll call a butterfly.

EVEN THE MOST BEAUTIFUL
HOME CAN BE VOID OF BEAUTY.

29.

THE NICEST GIRL ONLINE

*We've got 942 friends on Facebook, but when was the last time we
spent an afternoon sitting in High Park with one of them?*
—*Carl Honore*

It feels borderline blasphemous for a professional blogger to claim anything other than gratitude for the internet. It is, after all, the medium that offered me a career. It is the leveled playing field on which anyone with a computer and wi-fi can be heard from, listened to, read about.

It is a great tool.

And yet a tool is only as great as its user. A chain saw in the hands of Michael Myers yields vastly different results than a chainsaw operated by sculptor Matthew Crabb. One destroys, another builds.

I do not wish to destroy.

A bit of self-governing, then.

It is Tuesday, and I have just spent twenty-seven minutes on my phone. I timed myself, yes, because sometimes time is the only measure we've got. Time means priority. Time means love. Time means time.

I begin by checking my email. Sale alerts, deals, coupons. Delete, delete, delete. Wait. Do I need another pair of boyfriend jeans? Perhaps, yes, and especially for that price.

I click the link. "You deserve it," the

shop's banner proclaims, and I think, Yes, yes, I do. I am here, doing this living thing. I deserve denim, don't I?

I survey the selection and choose a perfectly distressed jean that is only slightly different from the pair folded in my left closet drawer. No, totally different. The seam, the color, the fade. So, so different. Add to cart.

And wait, while I'm ordering jeans, I might as well get it all out of my system. Do I deserve a few tees as well?

And then my virtual shopping cart is suddenly $189.70. But free shipping! A steal.

I stop. I have nearly spent more than a week's grocery bill on more things to wear, more things to toss aside, more things to replace in the near future. I click the browser's X. I will not succumb. A small victory, I think, and now I am feeling gloaty.

It has been six and a half minutes.

Now, Twitter. My feed is a cacophony of rants about a new vaccination bill, self-promotional links to e-courses promising happiness or fame or focus, and a few outliers talking about their dinner. I scan, scan, scan, and click on a link that shares twenty-two things I never knew about the movie *Clueless*.

It turns out I did not know twenty-two things about this movie, and I am pleased to report I am feeling wiser. Informed. I am riding the wave of knowledge and now have new fodder for dinner-party conversation at my fingertips.

Did you know Paul Rudd wanted to audition for Murray's role?

As if.

Thirteen minutes later, I am on Instagram scrolling through photos of sunsets and shoes, ice cream and sequins. My friend Jen is wearing a shirt that says "Here Comes the Sun," and I make a mental note to ask her where she found it. It looks vintage, I think, and I lament how long it has been since I've thrifted.

My other friend Caroline is in Iceland, and I make a mental note to look at plane tickets. Perhaps a springtime adventure is in order?

Still another friend is singing the praises of a new toy, and I am convinced Bee simply cannot go on living and playing without owning flat, angular tiles to create geometric domes from.

Amazon, then.

I have found them for a fair(ish) price, and this time I have succumbed. They will arrive in two days, cardboard evidence of my wasted time on the couch. Social media: 1. Erin: 0.

Twenty-seven minutes.

In words that have been attributed to David Foster Wallace, "It is named the 'web' for good reason."

I have justified, for many years, my time spent entrapped by the world wide web. After all, the internet is my cubicle; I would do well to know who's sitting in the corner office.

And yet twenty-seven minutes and a propensity for impulse purchases can catch even a spider if the threads are woven long enough.

A bit of detox, then.

Our society has a penchant for labeling things "detox" when they are simply measures to reset our self-governing abilities. It is not a diet, we say; it is a sugar detox. It is not vacation; I am participating in a productivity detox.

So, vacation.

It is early August. We have just landed in a tiny airport in Quito that smells of cumin and pipe tobacco, like a handful of smoked almonds your friend might hand you at a baseball game sometime in the sixth inning. You're not quite hungry for them, but they're there, and so they taste lovely.

TWO SOCIAL MEDIA DETOX STRATEGIES

001. Start small. Establish an easy rule you can stick to, like, "No more Instagram after 8:00 p.m." Master this, then add an extra challenge like, "No more Instagram or Facebook after 8:00 p.m." Then add in Twitter and perhaps Pinterest. Change 8:00 p.m. to 7:00 p.m., then 6:00 p.m., and on and on. Challenge yourself to go an entire day, if you'd like, without checking any social media networks. Can you make it twenty-four hours? Try forty-eight. Monitor your progress; see what feelings and habits surface. Consider asking a friend to hold you accountable and to celebrate what you've learned.

002. Delete all social media apps on your phone and fly to Ecuador.

Ken and I weave our luggage through security and customs while Bee drags a Bee-sized suitcase behind her. The Spanish I learned in high school is flowing back as I walk through winding hallways and peer past corners in search of a *bano* to *lavar mis manos*.

It is nearly midnight, and I have almost forgotten. As we wait for our driver, Washington, to pull the van around, I dig past our passports to find my phone. I will be deleting four apps this week: Facebook, Instagram, Twitter, and Pinterest.

With each click of the X on an app's upper right-hand corner, I feel farther from home. I am off the grid, in another country. I am stepping into a world that was created for me. I am stepping away, briefly, from the world I have created for myself.

Washington pulls to the empty curb in a big white van with pink dust collected on the hubcaps. "Welcome to Ecuador," he says with a wide smile as he gathers our bags. "You're going to love it here."

Facebook is the easiest app to delete. I don't keep an account personally, because I am a swirly mix of both privacy and sensitivity. What I read gets in, deep, and I suppose I don't want to have deep feelings about political conspiracies while eating my breakfast eggs before 6:00 a.m. I do keep a business account for my blog, but because a social media detox also means a week off from my online work, I have nothing to promote. Out of sight, out of mind. Easy peasy. Adios, Facebook.

The next easiest apps to toss aside are Pinterest and Twitter. I rarely use Pinterest on my phone, opting instead for the desktop version—for optimal viewing of women walking in front of bold pink walls, recipe ingredients on wooden cutting boards with a wedge of lemon nearby, Swedish-inspired interiors with gleaming white floors. There is plenty of newness to see here in the mountains of Ecuador, so it feels like a real-life Pinterest in a way (sans thigh gaps). I won't miss it a bit.

My hang-up, then, the crux of the detox, the reason for the season, is Instagram.

My friend Nicole often jokes that she orders food based on what might look best on Instagram, and we both laugh heartily until we notice the deep truth of it.

On a good day, I tell the truth on Instagram. I will take a photograph, albeit filtered, and I will say what I feel, what I think in that moment. I think of it as a gratitude practice, some of the time. A running list of all that I am learning to love, to accept, to embrace.

But on most days, I don't write what I think in that moment.

I write what I think others expect me to think in that moment.

There is a photo of Bee at a summer festival, dancing in front of a cigarette-smoking guitar player wearing John Lennon sunglasses. He is standing next to a vine-covered wall (Instagram requirement: check) on patterned tile (Instagram requirement: check) and Bee is twirling in a well-styled outfit (Instagram requirement: check) in plenty of natural sunlight (Instagram requirement: check).

It is a lovely photo, but it was not a lovely moment.

We were both hungry and I had just snapped at her for taking too long as we meandered through waves of street performers. We had passed by no more than six in twenty minutes, and she stopped to dance at each. I was selfish and impatient, and through that lens, I could not see how happy the musicians were to witness a toddler appreciating their music. I could not hear the beautiful melodies, the aching chords, the hard work and dedication and commitment each talented person was sharing for sheer joy, for our benefit alone. I could not accept the gift.

I could think only of a burger, and as I pulled Bee away from the sixth street performer, she cried.

This is not the Instagram caption I shared. I believe the caption I shared was "summer festivals forever," or something equally optimistic, airbrushed. Something you'd expect from the girl who once, before a keynote address, was introduced as "the nicest girl online."

Nice girls are just that, but they are not always kind to themselves.

It is this photo that I think of as we spend our week in Ecuador hiking in the mountains, tasting raw vegan tacos, enjoying massages from a shaman healer, and practicing new affirmations to implement upon returning home.

The first few days, I take a number of Instagram-worthy photos. There are adobe fireplaces with southwestern textiles, bountiful fruit stands in the market, mountain landscapes as the sun is setting. The light is perfect. The compositions are perfect. The inspiration is simply too much to capture, and look, did you catch that shooting star?

The photos fly into my phone's camera roll as I edit them, cropping them into squares to share when I return home from our trip. But over the course of the week, I stop taking photos altogether. I find that I can observe the beauty without capturing the beauty, and that I don't need to keep the memory for later. It is the moment and it is fleeting and it is lovely and that is that.

Novelist Toni Morrison once spoke of this. "At some point in life," she writes, "the

NICE GIRLS ARE JUST THAT, BUT THEY ARE NOT ALWAYS KIND TO THEMSELVES.

world's beauty becomes enough. You don't need to photograph, paint, or even remember it. It is enough."

We walk through the rest of the week the same way we entered it—wide-eyed and easily excited—but something has shifted. The initial excitement, the stimulation of a new and abundant environment, grows into something deeper.

I am calling it appreciation. I am calling it gratitude. I am calling it respect.

Once, on a walk through the hotel garden, Bee asks if she can pick a flower to take home.

"The flowers belong here," I say. "This is their home."

"But I want to keep it forever," she argues.

My answer is for her, but it is not at all for her.

It is for me.

"Sweet girl," I say. "It is not ours to keep."

30.

WHEN WE FLATTEN OUR BIGGEST SELVES

It is possible to be in love with you
just because of who you are.
—*Maggie Stiefvater*, Shiver

Some of us use social media to believe half-truths about others.

Others use social media to believe half-truths about ourselves.

"Which one?" Ken asks. "Navy or black?"

Tonight, Ken and I don our Sunday best to attend an anniversary dinner for our family friends Jim and Susan. I scrub the blue Play-Doh from beneath my fingernails and shave my legs; Ken chooses a tie.

When we arrive at the restaurant, our friend Andy, looking dapper in a suit, greets us with a heaping crate of Cracker Jacks boxes. He hands us two.

"Thanks, Andy!" I say, confused. "What're these for?"

He smiles. "You've really never heard the story?"

Thirty-five years ago, Jim proposed to his honey-haired bride in front of a VW van, after a candlelit picnic, with a ring from a Cracker Jacks box. As the story goes, he'd hidden a diamond ring in lieu of the plastic ring, and while the young couple dined on brie in the back yard, Jim's roommate

hungrily foraged in the pantry and then promptly pitched the box into the kitchen trash, declaring that the snack tasted worse than "caramelized moths."

"They kinda do, though," Andy jokes, ushering Ken and me to our seats at the table.

And as I tuck the small snack into my not-so-small bag, it strikes me how much I love this sweet proposal story. It strikes me how familiar it seems to us all.

When I think of the labels we give ourselves, of the roles we play, of the social media profiles we create to wrap up our great, big, bounding selves with a finite set of words and images, I think of this story.

When I think of the inherent value we possess, of the glistening creatures we were created to be, of the perfectly flawed diamonds we are—uniquely cut, uniquely sized, uniquely shining—I think of this story.

When I think of the ways we cheapen our identity, the ways we force our richest intricacies into small ideas, the ways we categorize each other in order to make sense of things—I think of this story.

And when I think of this story, I think of how we're all hiding in a Cracker Jacks box.

"Do you ever feel misunderstood?" an interviewer once asked me.

Doesn't everyone? Doesn't everyone feel like a diamond ring in a Cracker Jacks box, like they are both the gleaming rock and the kernels around it? That they are sometimes sticky, other times sweet, that there is a great pressure to make sense of their many flavors?

I do feel misunderstood, but the one doing the misunderstanding is me.

The one doing the misunderstanding is the one who wrongly assumes my social media profile and smiling square image must perfectly capture who I am. That my presence online must perfectly match my presence offline. That who I am is what I do, that my outsides match my insides, and surely if I'm sitting in a Cracker Jacks box I must be of little value.

Surely I am a plastic ring.

There is no truth in this belief. There is no truth in advertising, in the labeling of ourselves whether in the metal folding chairs at PTA or the white grids of Instagram.

We know better than to compare ourselves with others online. We know a Facebook feed, for most, is a glorified highlights reel, a round-up of our best moments, our funniest selves, our greatest champions. We know not to compare our worst with someone else's best.

But what do we know of comparing our self to ourselves? What do we know of comparing our richest reality to the one-dimensional screen? What do we know of flattening our identities so they can be cropped, manipulated, forced into one-liners and profile explanations?

What of that?

I don't think the most dangerous part of social media is the time we waste on our phones. I trust that we can keep this in check, that we can maintain focused communication with those around us and not become consumed by our devices.

(For those who can't, just know the number one dinner rule I keep among friends and family: the first person to interrupt a conversation to check their Pinterest feed, the football score, the flash sale on Instagram, etc., gets to pay the bill.)

Instead, I think the dangers of social media are far subtler than the distraction, than the addiction, than the habits we form by scrolling through screens multiple times a day. I think there is something far worse than the insensitivity of checking your phone in the middle of a conversation, when you unknowingly communicate to a person that what's happening on your screen is more important than their words.

I think social media has caused something far more dangerous, far more penetrating, a creeping issue that sneaks by daily, unnoticed.

Social media has encouraged us to crop out the contradictions in ourselves.

It has caused us to airbrush the parts of our lives we don't love about ourselves. It has caused us to sweep our personalities—whether too big or too small—under a Moroccan Pinterest rug in the name of a consistent social media presence. In the name of online optimism.

As a tastemaker, I have been taught that I have influence, that I should tread lightly when using this influence, that I should smile and nod and speak in a hushed tone. Careful now, don't offend. Don't rock the boat.

Perhaps you've been taught the same.

SOCIAL MEDIA HAS CAUSED US TO CROP OUT THE CONTRADICTIONS IN OURSELVES.

Perhaps you've been encouraged to use your circle of influence for a purpose—for entertainment, for information, for inspiration. Perhaps your phone number is starred as the go-to resource for homeschooling online or paleo meal plans or essential oils for beginners.

Perhaps people love when you share funny stories about your kids on Facebook, but when you get political, it's crickets.

Perhaps friends rave about your jokes, your artwork, your fill-in-the-blank, but when you admit to having a hard day, when you ask for help, when you reach out for something real and true and life-giving, your words fall on deaf ears.

And perhaps you think your diamond ring—your true self—is in need of a spit-shine. Or worse, that it holds no inherent value aside from the person you portray to others.

And perhaps you decide to hide in a Cracker Jacks box.

When we wrap ourselves in anything other than truth, in anything that doesn't acknowledge our authentic being, we risk hiding our inherent, God-given, life-affirming selves.

When we edit our biggest selves to fit into tiny profile images and Cracker Jacks boxes, we risk wishing away the parts of us that make us unique.

We risk dulling our diamonds in the name of cultural validation.

And then perhaps the most dangerous of all? We risk discarding other people's Cracker Jacks boxes—the ones we don't like—straight into the kitchen garbage bin.

After the anniversary dinner, after the carrot cake has been cut and the violinist has grown weary and the chiffon has turned itchy, Ken and I follow Andy to his car with the last of the decorations.

"Should we send the extra Cracker Jacks with Jim and Susan?" I ask.

"Nah," Andy says. "Susan hates the stuff. She only collects 'em for the surprise inside."

My current social media profile on Instagram reads "writer and mama in the Midwest." I identify with these titles, with these roles, with these small attempts to tame the wild gifts and fears and doubts that swim inside of me.

But so much of me is missing. So much of me is buried among kernels, cloaked in surprise.

I love afternoon thunderstorms in late July. I love fuzzy slippers and fireplaces, simmering chili and red wine. I love crisp sheets and old books and mailed postcards and cornfield sunsets. I love trench coats and city coffee and toddler lisps and kitchen messes.

I pick my cuticles when I'm stressed. I save my best perfume for someday (never). I sing off-key, terribly off-key, so badly off-key that my toddler has taken to correcting me—"Mom, I think you are saying the right words, but they are just not sounding like the right words."

I love most of this life, and I'm learning to love all of it.

I love most of me.

And I'm learning to love all of me.

There are four ways to measure a diamond's worth: color, clarity, cut, and carat weight.

There is one way to measure our own: yes.

Yes, you have inherent worth.

Yes, you are a bundle of contradictions.

Yes, you are a dazzling diamond inside a cheap box, and yes, the tension between the two is sometimes maddening.

Yes, it is tempting to crop out any contrast you see in yourself.

Yes, it is tempting to judge others by their boxes, their profiles, their rings.

But yes, we are all in the same box, wrapped in imperfect cardboard, carrying a great many kernels of ourselves.

On our drive home from tonight's anniversary dinner, Bob Dylan's "Forever Young" is on the stereo. Ken is reaching for my hand, asking if I had a nice time.

"Yes," I hear myself say. "Yes, I had a lovely time."

OO

31.

THE AGAIN-AGAIN-AGAIN DAYS

Even if I'm setting myself up for failure, I think it's worth trying to be a mother who delights in who her children are, in their knock-knock jokes and earnest questions. A mother who spends less time obsessing about what will happen, or what has happened, and more time reveling in what is. A mother who doesn't fret over failings and slights, who realizes her worries and anxieties are just thoughts, the continuous chattering and judgement of a too busy mind. A mother who doesn't worry so much about being bad or good but just recognizes that she's both, and neither. A mother who does her best, and for whom that is good enough, even if, in the end, her best turns out to be, simply, not bad.
—Ayelet Waldman, Bad Mother

Again, again, again!" Bee says. We are reading in the bedroom, and I have just finished telling her that she used to say "yellow" was "lellow" and "love" was "yove." When announcing her favorite color, she'd proudly squeal, "I yove lellow!"

and leave all of us grown-ups scratching our heads.

These days, these "again-again-again!" days are tiring, but in the good way. Bee will be four soon. Our days are filled with requests for brownies, requests for story

time, requests for the zoo, requests for her own zoo, requests for me to switch jobs to become a zookeeper at her own zoo so she and the monkeys can have ice cream after hours.

"At my own zoo, there will be sea urchins," she says. "I will measure them. They will weigh four hundred minutes."

We know of the many requirements of a parent's job. There are sticky banana-coated plates to wash and dirty socks to soak and endless tangles to brush out at day's end. There is the strawberry-cutting and the hide-and-seeking and the car-seat-buckling. The piggyback-riding and the sheet-tucking and the spill-wiping and the hand-holding. To say nothing of the hand-letting-go.

And then there's the socializing, the manners, the cultural enrichment outside of Daniel Tiger's jurisdiction.

It is enough to make you throw your hands in the air, to roll over on your back, to declare incompetence under the sheer pressure it takes to raise a child you pray does not become a jerk when grown.

This is a true prayer I have said, many a time. Don't let her be a jerk, God. Don't let me raise a jerk.

You can write that one in your Bible if you'd like.

Being a mother has been the most difficult challenge of my life, and it's not because of the workload or the fear or the barrage of hypothetical questions after 8:00 p.m. It's not even the bruised ego when she tells me my breath in the morning smells of dead dandelions.

It is the surrender. It is the failure. It is the knowing that I will never know, the accepting what I can never accept, the understanding that I will never understand what it means to perfect the gig.

In these again-again-again days, for many parents, the pressure is extraordinary. There is an immense amount of information and theory on technique and tradition, of

THIS IS A TRUE PRAYER I HAVE SAID, MANY A TIME. DON'T LET HER BE A JERK, GOD. DON'T LET ME RAISE A JERK.

articles floating around the ether proclaiming "One Hundred Things Your Toddler Should Know by Now."

It's a trap we all fall into, the temptation to measure our child's progress.

(It is, after all, the only way we can measure our own.)

The idea of letting down our kids, of providing them with an environment that is less than perfect, less than ideal, less than the standard—this is crippling for so many. Failing at parenthood means failing at life, doesn't it?

So we schedule more activities, we buy the best gadgets for the most enriching learning experience. We teach them to play the violin at three and a half, we teach them to read at two, we teach them to speak Mandarin at one.

We pack it all in.

I will measure them.

Throw everything at them and let's see what sticks, yeah?

They will weigh four hundred minutes.

And here we sit, lamenting our lack of balance.

I have heard it said that we are precisely the parents our children need. I have heard it said that our children choose us, like there is a great cosmic nursery in the universe's attic and the tiny babies are all fighting over who gets to live with Gandhi.

Perhaps they flip for it, and the rest of the babies just get us.

Some of us will inspire world peace and equal rights for future generations. Some of us might be really good at making cherry cobbler and beds. Some of us may earn Nobel Peace Prizes, and some of us might consider it a win if we don't sob and scream and threaten bedtime without dinner from three thirty on.

But on the best of days, we can hope that we have everything our children need from us. We have dedication, commitment. We have patience. We have grace. We have forgiveness. We have persistence, forbearance, creativity.

We have everything our children don't need from us too.

And yet.

We have love.

We have love, we have love, we have love.

What I have found about these things, about these characteristics—the love and the grace and the everything else—is that they fly right out the window when the kitchen gets hot. As soon as we begin watching the calendar, the clock (do you notice how he frowns, mostly?), we miss the adventure.

It is difficult to be patient when you are late for your six-year-old's piano lesson and the toddler wants to put on her shoes "all by my own self!"

It is difficult to offer grace when your preteen leaves his bike in the driveway (again, again, again) and you have a meeting in four minutes.

It is difficult to offer forgiveness when there is an emptied bottle of ketchup and a dog in the bathtub (*He's finger-painting, Mom!*) and the in-laws are on their way for prime rib.

It is difficult to be creative, to be forbearing, to persist when you cannot see a margin of time in your calendar. When you have not created space for laughter, for surprise, for ill-timed finger-painting sessions with a condiment-covered dog.

And it is difficult to accept all of it—the love and the grace and the everything else—when you have failed. When you have swatted a behind and it connected too hard and you had promised yourself you would never parent that way and now there are two sets of tears.

Busyness is a byproduct of our culture. It is the sacrifice we make for our religion of more, for our perfectionist tendencies, for our temptation to overschedule, overinform, overprovide.

But the answer is not to lower the expectations we have created.

The answer, I believe, is to live up to the expectations we have been created for.

Live up to the expectation that you are what your child needs. That your focus, your time, your attention, your failings—that these are enough. Live up to the expectation that your behaviors are being copied. Your reactions are being noted. Your forgiveness

BUT THE ANSWER IS NOT TO LOWER THE EXPECTATIONS WE HAVE CREATED. THE ANSWER, I BELIEVE, IS TO LIVE UP TO THE EXPECTATIONS WE HAVE BEEN CREATED FOR.

is being accepted. Your shortcomings are being acknowledged, understood, embraced. Your best is being called for.

Live up to the expectation that in these again-again-again times, you are enough.

What I learned from my seasons of more, of working for more and striving for better and yearning for perfect, is that even with the yearning, I fell short. I am not yet perfect. I am not fully actualized.

I never will be.

But in between the days when I am my worst, there are days when I am my best. There are days when I breathe through the tension. There are days when I do not roll my eyes when I see Ken has left his dirty T-shirt on the kitchen counter. There are days when I do not tap my feet at the post office. There are days when I do not see a homeless man on the side of the road and look the other way.

In these again-again-again days, I need Bee to see these moments. And if I am sending her to her room with the latest gadgets and toys, if I am shuffling her to and from dance lessons and toddler gymnastics and music class

before a quick drive through the burger joint, when I am too focused on the day to see this minute—this very minute—she will miss it.

And so will I.

Do you know the best things in life cannot be measured? Aptitude is not a perfect test score. Balance is not a perfect day planner. Creativity is not a perfect art sculpture.

The best things in life cannot be measured, but they can be learned, practiced, honed. Home is a good place to start—the place where we keep our junk drawer, where its contents find ways to spill out into the people who know us best, who have promised to love us at our worst.

In these again-again-again days with children in our homes, there are burning bacon and muddy paws and unrolled toilet paper, and there are yelling and do-overs, there are apologies and redeeming bath bubbles.

And there is great forgiveness, if we're lucky.

Immeasurable forgiveness, if we're even luckier.

Bee will be four soon. She is still talking of her zoo, of the monkeys and the after-hours ice cream, of the sea urchins and her grandest dreams, her wildest plans.

I know the feeling. These again-again-again days are my grandest dreams, my wildest plans. I do not want to waste them. I do not want to spend this weighty and precious time gritting my teeth in the name of productivity, in the name of pursuit, in the name of perfection.

And if Bee can bring imagination to the suffocating precision of math, of time, of counting and measuring and balancing this great untouchable life?

I will measure them.

Well, perhaps so can I.

They will weigh four hundred minutes.

And they'll be gone in a flash.

OO

32.

YELLING ABOUT THE BANANAS

*This contradiction, and this tension . . . it never goes away. And if you think
that achieving something, if you think that solving something, if you think
a career or a relationship will quiet that voice, it will not. If you think that
happiness means total peace, you will never be happy. Peace comes from the
acceptance of the part of you that can never be at peace. It will always
be in conflict. If you accept that, everything gets a lot better.*
—Joss Whedon, 2013 Wesleyan University Commencement Address

There are three people you do not want to receive a "whoa" from. Your dentist, while performing a routine root canal. Your inspector, while reviewing the electrical wiring in your new home. Your husband, upon your return from the hair salon.

I had asked for the hairstyle after taking an online quiz. I should have known better. "Does Your Hairstyle Fit Your Personality?"

it questioned, and the consensus was that no, my formerly tamed blonde bob did not reflect my personality. Instead, apparently, my personality called for something sort of spiked, something the color of merlot, something dramatic.

And dramatic it was. I very closely resembled a mahogany llama.

With the turn of the chair, the first

glimpse in the mirror, the stylist's smiling reflection, my internal dialogue began: Be brave. Don't cry. Smile wide. Tip 25 percent. Do.not.hurt.her.feelings.

And upon my arrival home, upon receiving Ken's "whoa," the same: Be brave. Don't cry. Smile wide. Do.not.let.him.know.he's. hurting.your.feelings.

This is the day I learned not to take online quizzes to find myself.

This is also the day I learned I was never really lost.

We go to great lengths to define ourselves.

We go to great lengths to search for wholeness, to make this match that, to compartmentalize our hearts so we can no longer be accused of hypocrisy. With shifty eyes and reckless souls, we whisper to ourselves, Don't be a mahogany llama disguised as a blonde bob. Don't be an average woman disguised as an online superstar.

Be a sinner, if you will, but don't be a sinner disguised as a saint.

I see now the error in this judgment. I see now how detrimental it is to embrace the parts of ourselves that make sense, that are tidy, that are justifiable, and ignore the parts of ourselves that are not.

A girlfriend once shared with me the theory about the three buckets we hold in our lives. One bucket contains our connection, another our vitality, and a third our contribution.

The theory goes like this: when one bucket is empty, the others need to be filled. When you're feeling lonely, alienated, and low on connection, boost your vitality and contribution. Take a walk, cook a nutritious meal, volunteer to bake cookies for the blood drive.

When you're feeling spent and low on energy, on stamina, perhaps you've been neglecting connections and contributions. Invite a few friends over for takeout and brainstorm creative projects. When you're feeling as if you have nothing to give, nothing to contribute, fill your connection and vitality buckets. Call a friend, journal, book a massage.

It's a life-changing message not because of the mechanics, not because of what each bucket holds or what each is missing or how you choose to fill them.

It is life-changing because it proves that we cannot snap our fingers to replenish what we have lost. In the great game of balance, what we are looking for is not often what we need.

I see now how my buckets ask not to be filled, not to be emptied, not even to be balanced.

My buckets ask to be accepted for what they are.

"One sandwich or two?" my friend Shannan says as she slices green onions for a tuna melt. We are sitting in her bright kitchen and the toast is browning in the oven, and I am staring at a collection of mugs, spoons, plates on the drying rack as I do my best to sort my words, to tell her the truth about the week I've had.

"Two for me," I answer. It has not been a good week.

Just yesterday I yelled at my toddler for not eating her banana, and then yelled at her for eating it the wrong way, and then yelled at her for not saving the second half for tomorrow's smoothie. We always do that! We always save the second half! You know that!

What?

I was a picture of irrationality, nagging a three-year-old as if she were being paid to perform duties, as if she were falling short on her performance review,

and *Young lady, if you do not cut that out, you are fired.*

I am not a yeller. I prefer communicating my demands in far more hidden, passive-aggressive ways. And so when I become a yeller, I know I have lost control of the ship.

Writers tend to live in one of two worlds. There is the murky water of their work, where, submerged, they spend the morning searching through seaweed to find a story—their story—to tell. And then there is the shore that awaits them when they rise from the deep—ringing ears, fuzzy heads—after a long bout of sentence structuring at the coffee shop.

This week, my shore is a bit of a mess.

I overscheduled, is all. I overcommitted while writing a book about overcommitting. This is not a line in the famed Alanis Morissette song, but it should be.

I have missed the birthdays of two nephews, opting to send them the cardboard-box-and-gift-receipt kind of love instead of the real deal. I have become largely absent from the lives of my friends this month, scheduling two international trips in a three-week span and spending the rest of my time flitting about the house looking for the travel-sized deodorant I remember hoarding last fall. On the shore, we have had takeout four times this week, because I simply cannot muster the strength to fry an egg for dinner. My bones are weary. My spirit is spent. I have been yelling about bananas.

You can imagine how difficult it has been to return to this book, then, when my shore is so very far from the depths of my work. I have a long way to swim, it seems.

Less me, more water.

"I am publicly lauded for championing a slow living movement, and I have found myself living fast," I say as I lead a metal spoon around the rim of my mug. "Isn't that hypocritical?" The tea bag chases the spoon as I chase my thoughts, and then it is quiet.

"Yeah," she says as she retrieves the toast from the oven. "So what?" She's speaking from experience, from her own attempts to fill in the contradictory corners of her life, to make sense of the lion in her den.

The heart of a woman is the best mirror you can find.

It's really quite simple, this universal truth: we feel empty on some mornings, tense in the afternoon, alone and forgotten and left behind by early evening. We spend our days searching to fill the wide margin between the person we are and the person we want to become.

We want answers, solutions, fixes, reasons for our tension. We cut out sugar. We quit drinking. We purge our closets. We buy more toys. We bake. We cry. And then we sit in the kitchen of a dear friend, and sometimes, when the tea is cold and the tuna melt is warm, we accept it all.

We accept the bundle of contradictions, the slew of tensions. We accept that they arrive as quickly as they're ironed out, wrinkle after wrinkle, until we throw our hands in the air and declare the day a domestic failure, an ill-fitting shirt.

Or we might choose to wear the wrinkled shirt anyway and enjoy it for what it is.

We are not our expiration dates. We are not 11.6 years or elevenish or maybe twelve if you round up. Life is not a puzzle to be solved. *We* are not a puzzle to be solved. Our dogs have eaten the pieces, after all.

Novelist Stewart O'Nan once wrote of this. "You couldn't relive your life, skipping the awful parts, without losing what made it worthwhile. You had to accept it as a whole—like the world, or the person you loved."

I am trying for this. I am failing at this. And I am no longer willing to call myself a hypocrite for the failings. I am no longer willing to feel this tension and to label it something, a judge dictating the sentence of another, the sentence of oneself. It is, simply, not that simple.

The whole of it never is.

I must be all of my multifaceted self. You must be all of your multifaceted self. We must allow every part of us; we must learn in great form, in human messiness. And we must accept it all. The good and the bad, the philanthropist and the philanderer, the street preacher and the drunk, the mother and the child, both dancing in the kitchen and singing on the sidelines.

The lion, the den. The dense jungle below and the relentless rain above.

Surrendering to the rain, to the discomfort, to the tension, surrendering to the contradictions and the failings and the hypocrisies, sounds like something I am familiar with.

Could that be the first whisper of a roar?

33.

We are all going, I thought, and it applies to turtles and turtlenecks, Alaska the girl and Alaska the place, because nothing can last, not even the earth itself. The Buddha said that suffering was caused by desire, we'd learned, and that the cessation of desire meant the cessation of suffering. When you stopped wishing things wouldn't fall apart, you'd stop suffering when they did.
—*John Green*, Looking for Alaska

The people who say everything happens for a reason haven't yet had anything reasonless happen to them," my friend says.

It is summer in the Midwest. There is crisp chardonnay and sandal blisters and ripe berry picking, and I am in the back yard at a friend's house, listening to the familiar *scrape, scrape, scrape* of the kids' skateboards on the driveway. We haven't seen lightning bugs in years, not since we were young. Bee is racing around to catch one in her hand, to keep as a pet, to carry home in a jar.

The season has felt heavy, like the sky has fallen a bit, like it's the lid of a Tupperware container and we're stuck inside, taking turns coming up for air. In my own small community, a girlfriend is dying of cancer

as her sixth-grade daughter learns about chemotherapy in health class. In my own small country, nine black churchgoers were gunned down by a white supremacist during a prayer service in their historic church. In my own small world, twenty-seven thousand children are dying every week from unsafe water and poor living conditions.

Everywhere we peek, there are miscarriages and mishaps and mistakes ending in divorce, and the older I get, the more I understand that none of us are immune to the reasonless.

And so here is my beef with surrender. What happens when we do it? What happens when we release the control, when we allow the inevitable, when we shed the protective layers we have tricked ourselves into believing we don? Who, then, do we get to blame for the wreckage?

Whose fault is it when a baby's heart stops beating? Who is responsible when the cancer spreads, when the brain tumor grows, when the hurricane wipes out neighborhoods and communities, when houses split in two and the neighbor's dog washes up in your overturned lilac bush?

"I got it! I got it!" Bee shouts. She has caught her lightning bug; her rosy cheeks and sweaty tendrils stand as evidence of the struggle. She is proud and begins rattling off her strategy, a beaming conquistador with cupped hands concealing the spoils of her battle.

"It's hard to catch a lightning bug," she says. "You can't see what you're looking for."

The Bible encourages a childlike faith. I do not yet know what this means, but I sometimes catch myself thinking it requires a profound sense of trust in your smallness. An acceptance of truth as it is today, as it is given today. The ability to look up and realize that faith is but a lightning bug—it is here and there and we need only wait long enough to see it, to trust long enough for it to light up and flit away, then light up again.

Who lives in the moment better than a child? Who is more trusting, more open to perspective shifts and upside-down ideas than ones who find solace in an imaginary friend? Who is more accepting of the reasonless, the senseless, the contradictions of life than the ones who question why some birds don't fly?

Why do bad things happen?

I do not know. I do not know why the sky, tonight, is black and dotted with the same stars that offer solace and rest for the grieving, while here I am, sipping chardonnay as Teitur plays "Poetry and Aeroplanes" from the back porch speakers.

You can't see what you're looking for.

I do not know why the same boiled water that softens the potato also hardens the egg.

I do not have a reason for the reasonless. I do not know that everything happens for a reason. I know simply that everything happens.

And tonight, Bee has happened upon a lightning bug and has named it Martin, and it is time for us to go home.

When I was younger, not yet tall enough to reach the kitchen counter, my mother would enlist me to organize her spice rack in the cabinet below. On Saturday mornings, with Bonnie Raitt and Rod Stewart music videos blaring from the dining room TV, she would flip chocolate chip pancakes on the skillet with me at her feet and a pile of thyme, dill, cumin in the corner as I considered my options for optimal compartmentalization. Shall I alphabetize today? Color code? Organize by height?

It was clear from a young age that I had a bright future in categorization, and I have not yet changed my ways.

Accepting that we are gray, that we are flawed, that we are a great many things, is one of the most difficult parts of today's information society. We are taught that knowledge is power, that what we do not yet know can be explained and placed in a box on the shelf, lid sealed until further notice.

We spend our time on social networks attempting to condense our personalities into tiny profile boxes, trying to verbalize intricacies within flattened screens.

Lawyer, mother, wife.

Artist and adventurer, sushi addict.

Yoga teacher seeking light.

I find comfort in a simple truth from the Bible, that there is only one Alpha and Omega. I think this means that we're off the

I DO NOT KNOW THAT EVERYTHING HAPPENS FOR A REASON. I KNOW SIMPLY THAT EVERYTHING HAPPENS.

hook in that department. That it is not our job to be Black and White, This and That.

I think this means we simply get to fill the spaces between—the many middles between the Beginning and the End.

We can inhale buttery popcorn and a chick flick today while rationing rice with turbaned women in Haiti tomorrow. We can fight the effects of rampant consumerism today and still purchase our mother a Christmas sweater tomorrow.

We can explore—in equal measure, if we choose—art and science. Laughter and sorrow. Truth and beauty.

We can lean in and lean out. We can conquer and retreat. We can teach and be taught.

We are not either/ors. We are both/ands.

OO

34.

NO BIGGER THAN A LOAF OF BREAD

Lucy woke out of the deepest sleep you can imagine, with the feeling that the voice she liked best in the world had been calling her name.

—*C. S. Lewis*

Through my seasons of slowing the pace, of subtracting expectations, of compartmentalizing and tidying and decluttering and choosing, I have made every attempt to manipulate my life.

I have made every attempt to tame my lion, to outrun it. I have made every attempt to pad my jungle—the leafy world of ambiguity—and I have made every attempt to control the style, the terms, the circumstances of my life.

I have chased more and I have chased less. I have lived large and I have lived small.

I have sped up, slowed down, traded up, pared down, built myself up, fallen down.

But have I looked up? Laid it down?

Perhaps we were never meant to change the pace.

We were meant to surrender it.

Still, we attempt the change. We clean out our garage. Every two years, at least. We quit our jobs, start new careers, cut our hair, welcome babies, buy juicers, switch schools, move to different houses, redecorate our kitchens, try acupuncture. We sign up for yoga. We diffuse lavender. We buy almond flour. We fluff our pillowcases, iron our blouses, send the kids to piano lessons.

We have done the work, we have made the change. There. Better. Ah.

But wait.

Our lion still prowls. He is still there. We feel him rumbling in our bellies late on a sleepless night. He stretches his wide paws and we feel him pushing on our guts, prodding our insides for something else. Something better.

Still?

More?

How many?

How much?

Yesterday, I heard him.

For the past year, Ken and I have been signing adoption papers.

Another plus sign.

I have been securing reference letters, financial statements, doctors' signatures. I have been interviewing caseworkers and agencies, scheduling home studies and notary visits. I have been reading writings from birth mothers and talking to adoptive mothers, asking advice. Something to ease the ambiguity. Something to satisfy the lion, to quiet the fear, to tame the unknown.

Are we safe? Are we secure? Can we handle it?

I text my friend the latest updates, sending smoke signals from my midwestern city to the beaches of LA. She has adopted twice herself and has become a great voice of reason, a great silencer of the lion.

"Are we going to be okay?" my message reads.

I am not asking her. I am asking God.

I drop my phone in my purse and walk downtown in search of a costume for Bee, something she'd described as a pirate bunny, but with a helmet so she could breathe underwater. I survey racks and racks of thrift-store gems—polyester prints from our mothers, fur coats from our grandmothers, Bakelite jewelry from our grandmothers' mothers. Nothing pirate here. Nothing bunny here. Certainly no underwater breathing helmets.

As I leave the store empty-handed, my mind wanders to the day ahead. It is a particularly busy one with errands and meetings; my mind is already fast-forwarding through the day: *Will I have time to grab a quick coffee before I head home? Do I have potatoes for a roast? Did I remember to postpone Ken's dentist appointment for next month?*

I almost miss it.

In the back alley, next to an old marquee

sign and an iron bed frame, I see a young gray cat. He is small, no bigger than a loaf of bread. He doesn't look stray, but he could be, and I see him stretching halfheartedly, claws in, eyes to the sun.

He looks ferocious.

He looks harmless.

He looks, a lot, like my lion.

He looks, a lot, like me.

He looks as if he spends his days laughing and lingering, failing and flailing. He looks as if he hunts and destroys on some days, builds and restores on others.

He looks as if he is a bundle of contradictions. A multifaceted true self, and one who knows it too.

He looks as if, right this moment, he has everything he needs.

So might we.

My friend's response comes in as I drive home; I hear my phone vibrate on the passenger seat.

"Define okay," it reads.

Define okay.

Define the lion.

Is he really a lion, fearless, prowling?

Or is he merely a contented house cat?

Is he after your soul or a simple lap of milk?

We get to decide.

We can turn molehills into mountains. We can seek to iron out any inconsistencies in ourselves, in others, in our world in an attempt to make sense of it all. We can puff ourselves up to make us feel whole, and we can manipulate the metrics we rely on to measure it all. We can throw it all at the lion and watch as he devours it like scraps of meat: the fast life, the slow life, the more, the less. We can exhaust ourselves with our offerings. We can keep tabs, keep pins, keep watch, keep score, keep track.

We can chase more, in the fast lane.

We can chase slow.

(It's still a chase.)

Or we can throw the metrics to the wind. We can pitch the scale, the ruler, the yardstick. We can look in the alley and see a cat, small and roaming, and we can finally understand what it means to accept this world for what it offers.

We were never meant to keep an eye on it.

We were perhaps only meant to see today.

A small gray cat, no bigger than a loaf of bread, stretching.

Claws in.

Eyes to the sun.

ACKNOW
LEDGMENTS

When you decide to write a book, when you decide to deplete yourself, you sit down at the corner table in a coffee shop and you look up from the blinking cursor to see a production of smiling baristas amid espresso steam. They are dancing. It is 7:14 a.m. This is the moment you will realize you are hopelessly wrecked and that your manuscript is due in six months and you haven't a thing to say.

But you will type a few more sentences, and you will backspace the rest, and you will work as they waltz, caffeinated with life. This will happen over and over again—you depleting, others dancing—and six months later, you email a manuscript with your eyes shut tight, wincing, crouching, a dog in a rainstorm. And there are people who will rescue you and pat you dry with a towel, and they will pick you up and say nice things, like *There, there. You're okay.*

Thank you, then, to the rescuers.

To my parents, who I often forget are everything. To Betsy. To the sisters who helped raise me, to my winding family tree—thank you for those stable, solid roots.

To the readers of the blog I began more than a decade ago—my goodness, you are still here. This is amazing and mindboggling; we are wrecked together.

To Stephanie, for your November email. To Karey, for your August and September ones.

To the ever-patient team at Zondervan. (Advance apologies for all those mixed metaphors; I'm working on it.)

To the baristas at my favorite eatery, for supplying me with black coffee and a waltz to witness. To my girlfriends, for bringing guacamole on the bad days and merlot on the good.

To Ken, the man behind the curtain. The reason, my reason, the wizard of Oz.

And to Bee, my yellow brick road. I'll follow you anywhere.

RE
SOURCES

FROM A TO Z, A FEW EASY
CHANGES TO SLOW YOUR LIFE

Attic Clean-out. Don't have an attic? Great, you're one step ahead of the rest of us. Take a nap, then move along. If you do have an attic, you already know what to do, don't you? Purge, sort, purge, sort. Give yourself time; the attic is where the hard stuff lives. Promise yourself a hot pizza later, but only if you donate the doilies.

Birthdays. If you have children, you have permission—if you like—to stop throwing over-the-top birthday parties with bounce houses and fondant cakes. Your children will not end up in therapy over this; they will likely end up in therapy over the time you kissed them good night wearing nothing but your clay pore-cleansing face mask.

Coconut Oil. Just grab a jar of this and keep it in plain sight. Eventually, you might use it, and then you'll feel even better about yourself. It's for cooking, cleaning, makes for a lovely face wash and/or body lotion, and have you not yet tried oil pulling? Google away.

Detour. The word *detour* sounds better than the word *interruption*, so I find myself redefining the setbacks in my life as detours, as little more than simple changes of plans. Burned the soup? Detour to pizza. Trip to the ER? Detour to perspective. Canceled appointment? Detour to free time.

Ethical Shopping. When possible, I purchase the bulk of my clothing or accessories

ETHICAL SHOPPING SITES

For Clothing
Accompany (accompanyus.com)
Cuyana (cuyana.com)

For Accessories
fashionABLE (livefashionable.com)
Tribe Alive (shoptribealive.com)

For Shoes
TOMS (TOMS.com)
Nisolo (nisolo.com)

For Beauty
LUSH (lush.co.uk)
Make Cosmetics (makebeauty.com)

For Home
Canvas Home (canvashomestore.com)
Local and Lejos (localandlejos.com)

For Kids
Wildly Co (wildlyco.com)
Walnut Animal Society (walnutanimalsociety
  .com)

from ethically sourced companies or socially responsible organizations. I have a short list here, but feel free to visit my blog for ongoing new favorites (design-formankind.com).

Formulas. Formulas are my go-to for practical slowing strategies. (You'll find my favorite math lessons sprinkled throughout this book!) I keep formulas in my head for everything in need of simplification: "Chicken + Any Veggie = Dinner"; "Toddler + Snack + Music = Tantrum Abated, for Now"; "Graphic Tee + Jeans + Turban = Instant Favorite Outfit in the Event of Unwashed Hair." If you use them enough, you'll memorize them, taking the guesswork out of daily details and leading you to more mindful ideals.

Gratitude. Gratitude for where you are, not where you hope to be, is the best virtue to practice on your quest for change. You are here, now. You have, thank goodness, been given all that you need for today.

Hydrate. If I'm in a bad mood, I'll drink a glass of water. If I'm tired, I'll drink a glass of water. If I'm hungry or stuck in a rut or feeling irritable and have a headache, I'll drink a glass of water. It's the greatest medicine I've found to date. Fill a pretty glass pitcher, throw a few slices of grapefruit in it, and leave it on your counter all day long. Cheers!

It Is What It Is. This is my favorite phrase when anxiety creeps in, when circumstances are beyond my control, when I am feeling misunderstood or angry or lamenting life. It is overused, yes, but it is good advice. It is true wisdom.

Just One. Big changes take small steps, and sometimes it takes just one thing to change the course of your minute, your day, your life. I believe in the power of one—setting the alarm one hour earlier, offering forgiveness one more time, stealing away for just one minute to yourself. Often it takes just one small thing, just one small thing that proves not to be small at all.

Knitting, or Something. Grab a hobby. Perhaps it's gardening with sunscreen on your shoulders, perhaps it's crocheting in the coffee shop. Maybe it's throwing pottery with the kids. Whatever you choose, carve out time to try something new, something different, something invigoratingly creative. It doesn't matter what it is, but it matters.

TYPE: BD-ML08N-OS
MFG: APOLIS - GLOBAL CITIZEN
ISSUE: STANDARD TOTE
ORIGIN: BANGLADESH PROJECT
FACTORY CODE: BD-LAT23.7099/LON90.4011
NGO: SAIDPUR BANGLADESH

Lavender. Lavender oils, lavender lotions, lavender candles. Whatever the medium, the scent sends you straight to relaxation station. I like to keep a few spritz bottles around my home to keep our spirits fresh and light. Fig+Yarrow's varieties are some of the best (figandyarrow.com).

Mason Jars. Of course you're not surprised. Mason jars are a staple in my home for storing dry foods (nuts, beans, grains, etc.) in the pantry and also for housing homemade beauty concoctions like organic body oil and sunscreen. My suggestion: The uniformity makes for a lovely, functional display in the kitchen. Go on, leave your food out on the counter!

Nap. I used to pooh-pooh the nap philosophy, but you know, sleep is some kind of elixir. It's free, and it's the simplest reset button on a hard day. The twenty-minute nap on the couch with the dogs is my favorite variety, but give me two minutes in a hammock while Bee is playing in the garden and I'll take it.

Options. Never, ever forget that this life offers options. It is easy to look around and see a sea of One Way, but just because we can't see an alternative doesn't mean it's not there. Discover something new on the regular. Feel trapped by your kid's school schedule? Research homeschooling. No longer want to use your accountant degree? Maybe you'd make a killer barista. We often hold the keys to our own cages. If you feel trapped by One Way, try a different key.

Pixie. If you're really feeling bold in your journey to less, might I suggest less hair? When I first made the chop, the shock quickly turned into freedom as I realized just how much I'd relied on my hair to make me feel feminine, beautiful, young, complete. A pixie and a smile exudes more confidence than any other look I've mustered, and hey, there's something to be said for taking a good thirty minutes off your morning routine.

Quiet Break. I do not meditate on the regular, but I do sometimes announce to my family that I will be taking a quiet break, which is a smoke break for nonsmokers. Five minutes of no noise in my bedroom, in the car, in the shower—or just last week in the bathroom stall at a friend's crazy overstimulating wedding—is all it takes. Breaks are good, breaks are worthy. Take them. Do not martyr yourself out of some good old-fashioned quiet time.

Read. Go to the library and pick an adventure off the shelf. Smell the pages, bend the spine, tap mindlessly on the cover as you lose yourself in the story. It's the only way, I'm convinced.

Soundtrack. Playlists are a staple in my home. There's the Kitchen Dance Party with Bee list, the Afternoon Pick-Me-Up list, and the Calm the Crazies list. Music is a quick and simple way to infuse a bit more slow into your day, and it's easy to create your own on a free app like Spotify (spotify.com).

T-shirt. My best style secret is that a classic tee, preferably in gray and white, is an essential item in your closet. Wear it alone to bed, with a blazer to work, with a skirt and fancy necklace to your niece's wedding, with your favorite pair of jeans to anywhere else you need to be. A linen blend makes for the most versatile piece, but your average everyday cotton version is ideal. Everlane carries my favorite socially responsible tee (everlane.com). (And it's just $15, FYI.)

Unbuttoned. I've been living life unbuttoned for a bit now, and it's a wonder. To be unbuttoned is to let your hair down, to resist the temptation to hold it in, to suck it in, to keep everything tight and tidy. The best things in life are the loose, the free, the light. You can practice next Thanksgiving over pecan pie. Let me know how it feels.

Vital? I'm often asking myself the question, Is this [blank] bringing vitality? Is this work opportunity essential to my version of success? (Almost never.) Is this purchase necessary to my life? (Almost never.) Is this activity fundamental to my parenting strategy? (Almost never.) Is this sacrifice crucial to who I seek to become? (Almost always.) Write down the word *vital* or *necessary* or *essential*. Tape it to your wall, if you must. Ask this question as often as you can.

Whole 30. While nursing Bee, I found she was allergic to milk and I'd need to cut out all dairy products. After researching many of today's most-relied-upon foods and their alternate effects on digestion, I embarked on a thirty-day challenge to "just eat real food." No processed foods, refined sugars, grains, or dairy products. The experience was transformative, and for a thirty-day kickstart to your own life change, I highly recommend whole30.com.

X. You know, the X on your web browser? Click on it today. Get offline and get outside. This is my answer to a slower day, each and every time.

Yoga. I don't know what happened exactly, but all of a sudden here I am, borderline obsessed with yoga. I like the slowness of the exercise, the growth that comes from strength and stillness. It teaches me to breathe, on and off my mat. My favorite method, so far, is Baptiste (baptisteyoga .com).

Zady. When I culled my wardrobe to thirty items or less, a good chunk of Zady items made the cut. With a focus on sustainability, slow fashion, and anticonsumerism, Zady believes that style can, and should, outlast trends. For quality classics in the home and closet, start here (zady.com).

FIVE METHODS OF
DECLUTTERING YOUR HOME

---

001. *The William Morris Method.* William Morris, a famed English architect, once established a golden rule for homekeeping everywhere: "Have nothing in your house that you do not know to be useful, or believe to be beautiful."

With this rule, you get to keep the mason jars (useful), the table lamp (beautiful), your grandmother's sewing scissors (useful *and* beautiful). With this rule, to your husband's detriment, you do not get to keep the 412 miniature, half-used bottles of hotel shampoo under the guest room bed. (Of note: Why no conditioner? Where has the tiny conditioner gone?)

002. *The Sick Dog Method.* I once shared this method with my blog readers, all of whom were surprisingly supportive and not at all offended by this slightly aggressive measure. But once, when Bernie threw up under my bed, I realized how little was worth salvaging down there. The grocery totes, the old college tees, the unused sneakers I diligently ignored (there was a brief running phase in 2009).

This is how the method works. Imagine your dog retching on your belongings, and if you wouldn't find them worth salvaging, you might as well do everyone (you, the dog, the old college tee) a favor and donate them now.

003. *The Toe Dip in a Cold Lake Method.* It's called this because you ease into it, slowly, surely, until the icy cold water hits your thighs and you know you're in deep.

With this method, you purge everything you think you won't use in one year's time. You stash all of it in unmarked bins (this is key) and put them in the garage, the attic, the basement, the neighbor's basement. Whatever. This is your safety net. The things still exist, so you're not quite ripping off the bandaid, but the chances of your actually digging through the garage, the attic, the basement to find an item are far less likely than your simply doing without.

And this is how you learn one of the main tenets of living with less: simply do without.

Next year, you'll have no idea what's in the bins. Your detachment will be complete. Go forth and goodwill it all.

004. *The Mother Method.* Invite your mother to stay with you in three days' time. Need I expand on this one?

005. *The Twenty Dollars Method.* I read this decluttering method in a psychology magazine once, and the trick is simple. Single out each item in a cluttered room, drawer, or closet. Ask yourself, "Would I pay at least twenty dollars for this?"

If the answer is yes, keep it or move it into "permanent storage." If the answer is no? Well, you know what to do.

P.S. During your decluttering efforts, you'll run headfirst into sentimental items: your grandmother's fur, a box of old trophies, that weird naked lady mug you gave your mother in third grade (I know nothing of this). Take photos of these items to keep in a designated hard drive, or if you're feeling extra virtuous, create an album of the photos. If you think this sounds like too much work, perhaps the items don't have much sentimental value after all.

From the Publisher

GREAT BOOKS

ARE EVEN BETTER WHEN THEY'RE SHARED!

Help other readers find this one:

- Post a review at your favorite online bookseller

- Post a picture on a social media account and share why you enjoyed it

- Send a note to a friend who would also love it—or better yet, give them a copy

Thanks for reading!